THE 100

Praise for *The 100*

"Practical nuggets of advice—from hiring slow to motivating high performers—with quick takeaways in downloadable form. You can also quickly access meaningful templates and guides to help implement these ideas."
> —**Tom Goodmanson, president and CEO, Calabrio, Inc.**

"Well-researched and insightful, *The 100* is a practical guide for personal and professional success. It is a must-read for anyone looking to build and grow their business."
> —**Stephen Yoch, attorney, speaker, and author of**
> ***Becoming George Washington***

"Quickly brings together the most important points of running a successful business. I will keep *The 100* close by for reference, inspiration, and affirmation on a daily basis."
> —**Steve De Vries, president and CEO, Showcore**

"Artfully captures Salonek's decades of leadership achievements and details repeatable steps that we all can take to improve our business results. Read the book, learn the secrets, and enjoy the fruits of winning in the marketplace."
> —**Steve Schmidt, president, AbeTech Bar Code & RFID**
> **Solutions**

"Clear, digestible, readily implementable action items with practical tips, specific recommendations, and supporting tools. It's a must-read for both seasoned and aspiring executives."
> —**Paula S. Weber, PhD, professor of management,**
> **St. Cloud State University**

THE 100

Building Blocks for Business Leadership

TOM SALONEK

AN AGATE IMPRINT

CHICAGO

Printed in the United States.

The 100
ISBN 13: 978-1-57284-196-3
ISBN 10: 1-57284-196-6
First printing: March, 2016

Library of Congress Cataloging-in-Publication Data has been applied for.

10 9 8 7 6 5 4 3 2 1   16 17 18 19 20

B2 is an imprint of Agate Publishing. Agate books are available in bulk at discount prices.

agatepublishing.com

To my dad Theodore, who taught me more about working with people than all the books I've ever read.

To my mom Jean, who encouraged me to go to college, which changed my life's course forever.

To my wife Linda, who has supported me for more than two decades. I'm lucky to have you at my side.

To my kids Theodore and Elizabeth, who are my joy . . . except when you're naughty and are on timeout . . . then, you're sort of a pain.

CONTENTS

CHAPTER 3: HIRING: THE FIRST STEP TO BUILDING A HIGH-PERFORMANCE TEAM

CHAPTER 4: LEADING AND GROWING TEAM MEMBERS

CHAPTER 5: OUTSMARTING AND OUTPLANNING THE COMPETITION WITH STRATEGY

CHAPTER 6: BRINGING OUT THE BEST IN PEOPLE

CHAPTER 7: GETTING THE MOST OUT OF OUTSIDE VENDORS AND CONSULTANTS

CHAPTER 8: MAKING PROJECTS SUCCEED

CHAPTER 9: LEADING OTHERS EFFECTIVELY

CHAPTER 10: MAKING MEETINGS WORK

INTRODUCTION

The art of living lies in a fine mingling of letting go and holding on.

—HAVELOCK ELLIS, *AFFIRMATIONS*

The 100 has been in the making since I founded my company, Intertech, in my basement in 1991. I don't mean that I've been actively writing the manuscript all this time, but I have been learning—both formally and through experience—about what it takes to run a successful business. Some of the ideas I once held have been abandoned after experience taught me a better way. Other strategies have been strengthened and honed based on invaluable feedback from my partners, advisors, and employees. I've also learned valuable lessons from graduate-level classes and from the esteemed professors and fellow entrepreneurs I've met through executive education programs at the Harvard Business School, the Massachusetts Institute of Technology, and the University of Minnesota's Carlson School of Management.

This book is practical and is meant for anyone leading a team or business. I've included lots of hands-on techniques, tips, and management strategies. The book also reflects my personal vision and values, both of which are essential to how Intertech operates. Again, let me be clear: I'm not saying my way is the only way; I'm simply saying that every business must be grounded in a clear vision and compelling values to truly build employee engagement, and, ultimately, success.

I'm certainly not a Stephen Covey or a Peter Drucker, but I have seen firsthand how effectively these strategies work at Intertech. Intertech has received more than 50 awards: for being one of the fastest-growing firms in America; for being one of the best places to work according to the *Star Tribune*, *Minnesota Business* magazine, and the *Minneapolis/St. Paul Business Journal*; and for excellence in our management practices. But the real proof of our success is that Intertech has an abundant roster of highly satisfied repeat clients, great employees, and a consistently profitable bottom line.

As an entrepreneur operating a successful IT development and training company, my experience includes work with many different employees and Fortune 500 companies, governmental agencies, nonprofits, and a good number of small- to medium-sized firms. In thinking about this book, I realized that despite their differences, all these organizations (including my own) are facing the same profound challenges.

The Internet of Things promises to transform (and is already transforming) every aspect of business and customer expectations. The global village predicted by Marshall McLuhan in *Understanding Media* grows smaller with each passing day, while social media makes it easier for a single unhappy customer to do extensive damage to your brand reputation.

On the employee side of the equation, things also are changing rapidly. Millennials are motivated much differently than employees of the past. Research says they will change jobs almost three times more than their baby boomer coworkers, are not interested in long-term employment, and are as equally committed to their work as to their employer (Lyons, 2012).

What does all of this mean?

Things are changing! The upcoming workforce is a generation unlike any other and will transform how we attract and retain talent. Our competition can come as readily from Bangalore as from our backyard. And a frequently uncertain economy makes forecasting challenging, at best.

Ironically, I believe all these changes are good in the long term. They force us to get better at serving our customers and employers, cultivating our employees (and ourselves), and understanding our markets. In essence, they compel us to build the strongest organizations possible to compete in the largely uncharted business waters of the 21st century.

In *The World Is Flat*, Thomas Friedman noted that to compete in the future, "We have to do things differently. We are going to have to sort out what to keep, what to discard, what to adapt, where to redouble our efforts, and where to intensify our focus."

I hope this book helps you to do just that.

NOTE ABOUT ONLINE RESOURCES

The 100 makes reference to more than 25 online resources to help you implement the book's ideas. Lessons that correspond with one of these resources are noted with this symbol: ☁

All resources are available for download at www.100theBook.com /downloads. For more details, see p. 158.

CHAPTER I

Living Your Best Life

KNOWING WHAT HAPPY PEOPLE KNOW

When I started Intertech, I was not particularly happy and neither—and not coincidentally—was my wife. Like many entrepreneurs, I was a classic workaholic driven to succeed with little regard to what it was costing my family, friends, or health. Luckily, I was young, healthy, and lucky to have an understanding wife.

I've learned a lot about the importance of happiness since starting my company. For me, happiness has a lot to do with healthy work–life balance. Dan Baker's book *What Happy People Know* is worth reading if you have not done so already. It debunks a lot of myths about happiness, such as the idea that money will make you happy. Based on plenty of solid research, this book explains that status symbols for happy people are "a happy family, good friends, and pride in their work."

I agree wholeheartedly. To achieve this type of deep happiness in my life, I had to step away and examine my core personal values, and then set goals and devise plans to realize those goals. Then I had to make sure I was consciously cultivating a work environment that would enable my employees to be happy too.

Why does this matter?

No matter how long you live, life is short. Your business should "give life, not take it," as Michael Gerber describes in his book *The E-Myth*. This requires planning, or "self-leadership," which includes identifying your personal values and your life mission, as well as setting goals backed by a plan to make them a reality. Once you've done this important work, you can begin getting your business into alignment with your deepest values. Not only will your business benefit, your employees will thank you, and your spouse and friends might actually forgive you for neglecting them in the pursuit of your dreams. I'm grateful that mine have!

TAKEAWAY: Happiness doesn't mean being in a good mood most of the time or experiencing the emotion of joy. Happiness is a way of life, an overriding outlook composed of qualities such as optimism, courage, love, and fulfillment. —DAN BAKER, *WHAT HAPPY PEOPLE KNOW*

2 UNDERSTANDING HOW VALUES PROPEL US FORWARD

I believe when we identify our deepest motivation—our values—and align our behaviors accordingly, we are more likely to achieve our goals. This is not quite as easy as it may sound. It takes time and focused effort to truly understand your deepest values.

For most of us, money is not enough to work late into the night to deliver for clients or make sacrifices for the good of our employees. While each leader's motivation is different (autonomy, security, stability, or something else), the power of values to motivate action is universal. They give us the reasons to do what needs to be done.

To discover my own deepest values, I imagined my funeral and what I hoped people would say about me after I was gone. Of course I wanted to be remembered as someone who loved his family and spent plenty of time (quality and otherwise) with them. This inspired me to begin taking annual fishing trips with my parents, which we did for more than a decade. We fished and laughed a lot. I learned more about my parents on those trips than I did in the 18 years I spent growing up on our dairy farm. Those memories became especially precious after my dad died in a farming accident a few years ago.

I also wanted people to remember me as caring for my business. I realized that caring about my business really means caring about my employees. If I deserved balance, they did as well. This motivated me to ask employees what would help them achieve better work–life balance. Their candid feedback spurred our giving three-month sabbaticals for every seven years of service. We also began seeking work that would allow our consultants to work from home at least part of the time, and offering a $1,500 budget to new employees to equip their home offices. (Values don't mean a lot if you are not willing to put money behind them.)

Values bring meaning to our lives and our goals. They also serve as guiding principles when executing the work plan of goals.

TAKEAWAY: It's not hard to make decisions when you know what your values are. —ROY DISNEY

3 CREATING A ROAD MAP TO REALITY

Goals transform vision to reality. But there's a caveat. To be effective, goals must be SMART: Specific, Measureable, Achievable, Realistic, and Timely. Many of us make long-term goals; specific short-term goals, however, are responsible for achieving our long-term goals. Writing your goals down is equally essential.

Need convincing? Consider a study by Dominican University professor Gail Matthews. In her research, those who wrote their goals down, made an action plan, and communicated the goal to others were twice more likely to achieve their goals than those who just thought about them.

Here are a few practical tips that I've learned about setting goals and action plans to achieve them:

» Write down your goals and then allow a few weeks to pass, to test your conviction. Why waste time developing plans and working to achieve goals that are not that important to you?

» Break your goals into manageable daily actions.

» Look at your goals weekly or even daily. Post them where you can see them constantly.

» Always aim high and include dates. A goal without a deadline is just a dream.

For more about goals, read *Think and Grow Rich* by Napoleon Hill and *The Magic of Thinking Big* by David Schwartz. Why bother to read about goals? Goals cannot be achieved in a vacuum. You need assistance—and inspiration—to achieve them.

TAKEAWAY: Always remember that your own resolution to succeed is more important than any one thing. —ABRAHAM LINCOLN

4 ENVISIONING YOUR FUTURE

What do you want your business to look like in 10 years? Who are your ideal clients? How many employees will you have in 10 years and, more importantly, what kind of people will they be? Once you have the answers figured out, close your eyes and try to visualize how this looks. Picture your office; imagine your employees interacting with those ideal clients. Think about the rhythm of your day and how you will look, act, and feel at work and in all other areas of your life.

Taking time to develop and visualize specific scenarios in response to precise questions will help you shape the future of your business and your life. As I mentioned in the previous section, having clarity around your personal values, life mission, and goals will make it easier to visualize the future for your business. Your personal and business visions should support—not contradict—one another.

Don't misunderstand. I am not consulting tarot cards or crystal balls to run my business or my life. My advice is based on solid and astounding research into the power of visualization. Take, for example, the story of accused Russian spy Natan Sharansky. He spent nine years in solitary confinement and used the time to visualize himself as a world-champion chess player. This is a pretty lofty goal for a guy without an opponent, much less a chessboard. In 1996, he beat the reigning world chess champion.

Even more incredible, at least to me, is the Cleveland Clinic study on visualization in which the control group went to a gym and did regular strength training (Ranganathan VK, 2004). Another group of similarly fit people simply visualized doing strength training. The results: visualizers achieved more than half of the physical strength results as the control group, without ever setting foot in a gym or touching a barbell.

Visualization is not magical thinking. It's a proven scientific method used by athletes and many others to improve performance and achieve desired results.

TAKEAWAY: Analyze the past, consider the present, and visualize the future. —THOMAS J. WATSON SR.

☁ DI

5 DOING LESS EQUALS LIVING MORE

Ever heard the saying, "We're human beings, not human doings"? You don't have to be a Zen master to understand the wisdom behind this message. Yet many people, including organizational leaders at the highest career levels, are caught in activity traps that waste time and energy and accomplish astonishingly little. While ancient wisdom tells us to value our time and to remember to focus on the joy inherent in every passing moment, 21st-century technology is making it possible to simultaneously accomplish a lot (including many mundane but "must-do" tasks) and still have plenty of time for all the other things in life that matter.

Several books have helped me master the art of personal time management, including almost everything ever written by Stephen Covey. I'd also like to credit a practical little book called *Less Doing, More Living* by Ari Meisel, and *Give and Take* by Wharton Professor Adam Grant. The ideas I'm sharing here (and in the following sections on giving, tools, and email) were found in those books, which I highly recommend you read as soon you find the time!

Managing time really means being in control of your schedule and your life. For me, this means using Covey's example (in his book *First Things First*) of the metaphorical big rocks going to my bucket first, with sand filling out the rest. My "big rocks" are meetings, daily huddles with my partners, time with my family, and exercising. My "sand" is whatever comes up during the day like phone calls, informal discussions, or day-to-day to-dos.

Big rocks get top priority in my schedule. To keep it simple, I designate Mondays for meetings, Tuesdays and Thursdays for working from home, and daily 15 minute huddles (phone or in person, depending on where I'm working that day) in which I touch base with my partners to make sure we're all on track (see 88, page 137, and 98, page 157, for more about huddles).

If you adopt my strategies, be prepared for a little good-natured ribbing from colleagues who can't understand how you spend three days a week in the office and still run a successful company. Learn to smile and explain that the secret is working smarter, not longer. And make sure you apply the same standard to your employees: judge them on results and not the number of hours they keep their chairs warm.

TAKEAWAY: Do not squander time, for that is the stuff life is made of.
—BENJAMIN FRANKLIN

6 FINDING BALANCE BETWEEN GIVING AND TAKING

Nothing can derail your schedule faster than unexpected interruptions, such as sales pitches masquerading as "partnering conversations." On the other hand, sometimes responding to appeals from others is simply the right thing to do. Sometimes we give because it helps others. Sometimes we give because it helps us. Learning to harness the benefits of giving while minimizing the costs—both in terms of time and money—is what the book *Give and Take* by Adam Grant is all about. Grant writes:

> For generations, we have focused on the individual drivers of success: passion, hard work, talent, and luck. But today, success is increasingly dependent on how we interact with

others. It turns out that at work, most people operate as takers, matchers, or givers. Whereas takers strive to get as much as possible from others and matchers aim to trade evenly, givers are the rare breed of people who contribute to others without expecting anything in return.

While many self-sacrificing givers are perceived as "chumps," others rise to the top of the success ladder because they contribute to others. Like most things in life, it's all about finding the right balance and using proven strategies to cope. For example, when others approach me about "partnering" but are really just selling something, I ask them to talk with me when a real deal is in hand. In short, I don't waste countless hours discussing a "business venture" that, in the end, will not provide any real business benefit to my firm. If there's a real opportunity with real money at stake, we define our partnership.

When thinking about my company's culture, I definitely want to encourage teamwork and cooperation among employees. This must be balanced with meeting individual deadlines and client expectations. Leaders can assist extreme givers by helping set boundaries.

At Intertech, we financially compensate employees who have agreed to work overtime to help others. Along with the comp, we provide guidelines about when help can occur. We need to ensure that helping does not interfere with the helper's primary work responsibilities. We also require that the help only consists of mentoring, not actually "doing" another employee's work.

Helping givers see the big picture, such as how the company is performing against goals on a quarterly basis, connects their individual choices to the company's mission. Discussions about meeting clients' expectations also can be helpful.

TAKEAWAY: No one has ever become poor by giving. —ANNE FRANK

7 USING TOOLS TO MAKE LIFE EASIER

As a former programmer and the founder/owner of a software consulting and training company, I admit I might have a bias in favor of technology tools. Even so, I've found a few excellent tools that have dramatically increased my productivity that I'd like to share with you. They're easy to use and, best of all, can save you precious time while increasing your ability to remember and act on discussions or ideas that otherwise might be lost in the blur of a busy day or week.

Evernote lets you take notes in any form, including text, phone calls, pictures, drawings, scanned documents, and web pages. Think of it as a catchall container where you can collect information, easily find it later, and organize it to present to others. Evernote is free, has no storage limits, and works everywhere. It syncs across all types of cell phones, tablets, and computers. The web-clipper function, which works with Gmail, Chrome, and Firefox, allows users to click and save anything interesting found on the web. In *Less Doing, More Living*, Ari

Meisel considers Evernote the heart of his "external brain."

My other favorite technological tool for personal effectiveness is Livescribe, which is a paper-based computing platform that includes a smart pen, a journal, and a software application that allows you to easily capture, use, and share information. At its most basic, Livescribe translates written notes and syncs them to Evernote. It also can "hear" conversations and allow you to replay them after the fact in case you missed something in your notes.

Finally, SugarSync syncs files between your laptop and desktop computer and allows you access to documents on your phone and iPad.

Use these tools to increase productivity. They also might make you seem more interesting at parties (assuming you hang out with tech types too!).

TAKEAWAY: If he wishes to make his work good, the craftsman must first sharpen his tools. —CONFUCIUS

☁ D2

8
MAKING EMAIL MANAGEABLE

Love it or hate it, email is a major part of our 21st-century existence. If you're like most leaders, you probably receive a lot of email: some urgent, some essential, and some just plain old junk.

My approach to email is fairly simple, but I do have one cool tech tool to recommend.

Think of email as a hot potato. Ideally, you only want to touch it once and for as quickly as possible. That means responding to quick items as soon you open and read the message. Boom: done and done!

If the email pertains to something you need to do in the future, make it a "to-do" in Outlook or, better yet, use an automatic email reminder service called FollowUp.cc. It could not be simpler but will save you from forgetting to follow up with someone or do something important in the future. When sending a message to someone whose response is required by a certain date, bcc FollowUp.cc, including the number of days you would like to pass before the service sends you a reminder (e.g., twodays@followup.cc). When that time frame has passed, you will receive an email reminder with your original message attached.

FollowUp.cc also creates calendars and even has a snooze function so reminders can be deferred if necessary. This cool tool is sort of like an old-fashioned personal assistant (Don Draper never had it this good!), but one that gives you complete control.

For some, email has become an unmanageable monster. Along with making it a goal to touch email once:

» Liberally use your email's spam feature.
» In programs like Outlook, turn an email into a to-do by dragging it to the To-Do button, so you can deal with it later.
» Use email folders and features as a way to organize and declutter. Here again, programs like Outlook have a Quick Steps function that can file the email with a single mouse click.

» Save important emails to Evernote by forwarding them
to your personal @evernote email address. Then delete
them from your inbox.

» Organize travel using the mobile app and website TripIt.
You can forward any email confirmations from airlines,
hotels, or activities to TripIt, which will then create a full
itinerary for you.

**TAKEAWAY: The great enemy of communication, we find, is the illusion
of it.** —WILLIAM HOLLINGSWORTH WHYTE, *FORTUNE* MAGAZINE

9 BEING A PRODUCTIVITY ROLE MODEL

As mentioned in takeaways 1 and 2 (pages 21 and 22,
respectively), I believe it's important to align your personal
values with your business. Since achieving a healthy work–life
balance supports my highest values, I strive to model productivity techniques and then embed them within my organization.
While a bit of an adjustment for new hires, over time, most of our
team members say they appreciate the efficient way meetings are
run and decisions are made.

The key component is each team's daily meeting huddle,
usually right before people head home for the day. A huddle,
borrowed from the Scrum method of software development, is a
quick 15-minute standing (sitting encourages rambling) recap of
anything important or pending based on that day's business. We

focus on results, not process, and give team members on the front lines parameters for making decisions on the fly. This keeps business from bogging down and lets everyone play a more significant role in the firm.

When working with assistants, delegating is done in an *if/then* fashion. For example, I may say, "Shoot for a board meeting with everyone attending at our office on the week of the 20th. If that doesn't work, try the week of the 27th with some people dialing in for the meeting. After the date is set, send a meeting invite to all with location info and dial-in instructions."

TAKEAWAY: As a leader, it can be tempting to get down into the weeds. Resist this temptation.

10 FRAMING DECISIONS

When making decisions around life or business, frame decisions in the future tense. For example, for business, when considering a new goal, policy, or idea, ask: "Will this new *(fill in the blank)* still make sense when we are two or three times bigger?" Doing this helps ensure the goal or decision takes you one step closer to the long-term mission.

TAKEAWAY: Framing questions in a future tense helps leaders think of the long-term, more strategic impact of a decision.

HARNESSING THE POWER OF EXECUTIVE DASHBOARDS

As a lifelong Minnesota resident, I honestly can say I love it here . . . except in January and February. That's when my family and I—and many of our fellow Minnesotans—head to warmer climes for as long as we possibly can.

While we appreciate escaping from winter's deadly grip, I cannot lose my grasp on what's happening at Intertech while I'm physically away. Thanks to executive dashboards, that never happens.

Intertech's executive dashboard ties into our CRM (Customer Relationship Management) and accounting systems and provides a clear view into sales, profits, inbound leads, and other leading performance indicators. Our entire leadership team reviews the dashboard on a regular basis, which allows us to avoid unpleasant surprises and difficult conversations. We all have the same facts at the same time, no matter where we are at any point in time.

Best of all, the executive dashboard empowers us to make changes—early—whenever we detect a trend moving in the wrong direction.

TAKEAWAY: Keep your eyes on the road and your hands upon the wheel. —THE DOORS, "ROADHOUSE BLUES"

CHAPTER 2

Using Employee Engagement to Outperform Competitors

12 UNDERSTANDING WHAT ENGAGEMENT IS

Engaged employees are "in the zone," to use a sports metaphor. That's the place where things feel right, are working optimally, and where the future looks promising. Fostering employee engagement probably is the smartest thing a business owner can do to build a winning business. Why is engagement so important? According to a 2013 Gallup poll, companies with highly engaged employees experience

- » 22 percent higher profitability
- » 21 percent higher productivity
- » 48 percent fewer safety incidents
- » 37 percent less absenteeism

So the benefits are clear, but building employee engagement is about doing a lot of little (and some big) things consistently and well. That's what this chapter is all about.

TAKEAWAY: Engaged employees deliver more profit, productivity, and fewer problems. It makes 110 percent sense to take time to understand and, more importantly, to create an environment of engagement.

☁ D3

13 UNDERSTANDING WHAT ENGAGEMENT IS NOT

Forget the "cool" workplace clichés. Employee engagement has nothing to do with gimmicks like foosball tables, Nerf guns, or "beer 30" every Friday afternoon. Dogs, unless they're of the service variety, have no place at work.

Fortunately, allowing employees to bring their dogs to work, wear tattered jeans, or play with Nerf guns in the halls has nothing to do with employee engagement. Those are gimmicks frequently employed by tech startups in the Internet boom days to attract top programmers and to distract them from the all-too-often fleeting real benefits (like salary and stock options).

There are better ways to build engagement with employees, which this chapter will describe in detail. For now, just remember that building engagement is not expensive and it pays off big time. When companies can pair engaged employees with engaged customers, outcome-oriented business performance increases by 240 percent over companies with neither group engaged (Gallup, 2013).

TAKEAWAY: End-to-end engagement not only increases business performance, it dramatically reduces issues and hassles with employees and customers.

14 LEVERAGING TEAMWORK

In his book, *Give and Take: Why Helping Others Drives Our Success*, Adam Grant says that "organizations have a strong interest in fostering giving behavior." I believe this is spot-on. "A willingness to help others achieve their goals lies at the heart of effective collaboration, innovation, quality improvement, and service excellence. In workplaces where such behavior becomes the norm, the benefits multiply quickly," he also notes.

Intertech consultants truly embrace the "one team, one dream" philosophy, and our company continues to grow and thrive as a result. We do not tolerate ego-inflated superstars who think only of themselves, to the detriment of customers or fellow consultants. We only hire professionals who understand the value of pulling together, like crew members of a rowing team, with corresponding positive results.

Of course, sometimes consultants need to focus on a particular project or deadline and are not readily available to give assistance when asked. We encourage our consultants to consider the feelings of their colleagues in these situations and to share why they are not available. A statement like, "I would like to help you, but my customer is expecting my project tomorrow. I don't want to disappoint him," is a lot better for team morale than, "Are you kidding? I don't have time to help you!"

TAKEAWAY: It's easy to stop one guy, but it's pretty hard to stop 100.
—JACK STACK, *THE GREAT GAME OF BUSINESS*

15 USING GOAL ALIGNMENT

McKinsey Quarterly recently published a study that showed a clear relationship between a company's organizational health and its financial performance. Good organizational health relies in part on everyone being in alignment—both with the company's goals and each other.

Getting everyone on the same page should begin the first day someone joins your company. At Intertech, we provide an employee checklist during orientation that includes our overall financial and strategic goals, along with how the new employee fits into that picture. The goal is to set expectations early and, most importantly, to help employees gain a sense of ownership.

Setting the stage on day one is just the beginning. It's also critical to work with employees to set achievable goals, provide training and support, and hold them accountable. Equally critical is regular communication about the company's progress toward its financial and strategic goals. See Leading and Growing Team Members (page 65) for more information about this important topic.

TAKEAWAY: Just as your car runs more smoothly and requires less energy to go faster and farther when the wheels are in perfect alignment, you perform better when your thoughts, feelings, emotions, goals, and values are in balance. —BRIAN TRACY

16 BUILDING COWORKER TRUST

Building trust among coworkers takes time and requires opportunities for people to get to know each other as people. Personal sharing, frequently the casualty of a busy workday, should be fostered in appropriate ways. There are simple things you can do to model important relationship building, like asking your team members about their weekends.

Intertech sponsors a number of social events that allow our consultants to have fun and get to know each other. Volunteer outings, company parties, and Friday summer barbecue lunches (families and friends are always invited too) are among the ways we hope to cultivate coworker trust. We also encourage our consultants to come up with their own ways of connecting, such as the occasional golf outing and the ever-popular fantasy football league.

Some might shake their heads and wonder why we allow "frivolous" activities to happen during work time. Yet, what might seem frivolous on the surface actually yields powerful dividends in the form of employee cooperation, teamwork, and positive morale. People who like, respect, and most importantly trust each other can work together as a highly functioning team, one that can have disagreements without questioning each other's intent or becoming vindictive. It's also a lot more fun to work with people who get along and enjoy mutual respect!

TAKEAWAY: Trust is the glue of life. It's the most essential ingredient

in effective communication. It's the foundational principle that holds all relationships. —STEPHEN COVEY, *THE 8TH HABIT: FROM EFFECTIVENESS TO GREATNESS*

17 RECOGNIZING INDIVIDUAL CONTRIBUTION

Ask anyone at Intertech what they like best about their job, and you'll likely hear a variation of "I enjoy solving problems for clients." I suspect many people derive the most work satisfaction from what they achieve and the creativity they use in the process.

We've consciously created a culture that celebrates our consultants' wins, particularly when they happen as part of a team. We also expect everyone to take ownership for productivity. Ask me when any of my direct reports arrive, leave, or work from home, and I'll readily admit that I don't know or care. I care about results. At the very least, they need to create awareness of the business impact of their daily heroics so management can provide support—and kudos—as necessary.

So, while individual contributions are lauded and rewarded financially, I firmly believe that the overall work environment must put the most value on empowering people and encouraging them to support each other. At the end of the day, most bright, hard-working people want to be part of a firm that recognizes success of the business is more important than any single individual.

TAKEAWAY: Happiness lies in the joy of achievement and the thrill of creative effort. —FRANKLIN D. ROOSEVELT

18 KNOWING MANAGER EFFECTIVENESS

Being a great leader may be one of the hardest jobs on the planet. While developing solid management skills definitely plays a part, I also believe good management is as much about who a manager *is* as what he or she *does*.

Setting a great example for others starts by simply being an authentic human being who is not afraid to try something new or make a mistake. Good managers take responsibility for their actions and admit their own mistakes. By demonstrating ethical behavior, they create an environment where it's OK to be wrong and, most importantly, where things get done.

Managers at Intertech are more like coaches, helping their direct reports see their part in the big picture. They promote collaboration and teamwork, and they work to promote continuous improvement through training. Our managers know how to influence, engage, and inspire commitment from others. But they're also cheerleaders, taking great pride in the accomplishment of their team.

TAKEAWAY: Managing can be seen as taking place in a triangle where art, craft, and the use of science meet. —HENRY MINTZBERG, *SIMPLY MANAGING: WHAT MANAGERS DO—AND CAN DO BETTER*

19 TRUSTING IN SENIOR LEADERS

Senior leaders at Intertech are expected to behave like our managers: lead the way, admit mistakes, and communicate that it's OK to be wrong. In my experience, this is the only way to create an environment that fosters creativity, innovation, and risk taking. It also inspires people to continue working together, year after year, in the pursuit of common goals.

Intertech partners also model how a highly functioning team can disagree without questioning one another's intent. In other words, we trust that each partner has the best interest of the firm in mind, even when we disagree about which path to follow. By trusting each other, our consultants sense it's safe to trust us too.

Of course, trust is built over time and requires honest, frequent communication. We must demonstrate we have the ability to think strategically and know how best to leverage our company's competitive advantages.

Competent leadership means little if we do not share what's happening with all of our people. Letting employees know we have realistic plans to achieve results and the drive and initiative to see them through is the foundation for building trust in senior leaders. All of this, combined with humor and humility, helps to keep us all working together as a harmonious team.

TAKEAWAY: An easy way to do the right thing is to think of what you'd want in a leader or what you respect in other leaders: honesty, humility, clear and objective goals with fairness and accountability, and recognition for a job well done.

20 FEELING VALUED

In this section's takeaway, funny lady Tina Fey makes a good point . . . up to a point. Empowering our people to make independent decisions and to organize their work lives in the way that suits them best is how we roll. But we also work hard to make sure they and their many contributions get the recognition and respect they deserve.

Intertech has received more than 20 awards for being a great place to work over the years, and we've been honored with first place on a list of incredibly impressive companies. As the founder and CEO of Intertech, I'm always humbled and delighted when these awards are conferred. It feels fantastic to be recognized for running a great company.

But most of all, I'm deeply satisfied to know that our employees feel valued here. Without them, Intertech would still be a faint dream in my mind. Our people are the lifeblood of this organization, and we take—and make—many opportunities to let them know we could not do it without them.

TAKEAWAY: In most cases, being a good boss means hiring talented people and then getting out of their way. —TINA FEY, *BOSSYPANTS*

21 HAVING JOB SATISFACTION

Imagine a depiction of concentric circles representing varying levels of job satisfaction. Enjoying the actual work at hand and a having good relationship with one's direct supervisor would be at the very middle of these circles, because they are the central tenets to job satisfaction.

If your goal is to engage employees, you must start at the core and then work outward to address things like career and personal development, work obstacles and extrinsic rewards, and finally, senior management and overall confidence in the firm.

It only makes sense; our day-to-day work is what consumes most of our time and energy. Getting the fundamentals right—the blocking and tackling—is most critical to employee job satisfaction and overall engagement in the business. For us, this means having systems in place, such as Dale Carnegie's Key Result Areas (see 36, page 70, for more information), daily huddles, monthly meetings, and a weekly e-newsletter to encourage consistency, communication, and teamwork. We strive to ensure that each of our consultants can engage their respective talents in interesting work, and that they are able to work in a friendly and respectful environment, with low stress.

All of this is not to say that compensation doesn't matter. It does, which is why the final takeaway in this chapter on employee engagement is all about benefits and pay.

TAKEAWAY: For job satisfaction, a job's core needs to be the focus, not the frills. If there's free beer every Friday, but the employee's job is monotonous and the manager's a jerk, frills don't matter.

22 KNOWING BENEFITS AND PAY

Money doesn't matter, unless you don't have any. As much as I believe in the importance of creating a first-class work culture filled with intrinsically motivated people, I also understand that most of us also work to pay for our life. That's why we pay slightly higher wages than the market dictates, provide bonuses, and offer an additional financial reward system based on how well the firm does as a whole.

Money aside, benefits are a crucial part of the overall compensation package at Intertech. Things like health insurance and 401(k)s are a given, of course, but we also provide benefits that employees might not expect but truly appreciate. This is where creativity comes into play. Surprisingly, offering unique benefits that really matter to people doesn't have to break the bank.

For example, Intertech employees are given tremendous freedom to structure their work environment as they see fit. Some choose to work in the office, or at a client's site, for nine hours a day, nine working days in a row, which then gives them one four-day weekend per month without having to use vacation days. Others prefer to work from home, particularly during the winter. As I mentioned earlier, we also give a $1,500 benefit for new employees to make any necessary home-office purchases.

As shared earlier, another popular benefit is our sabbatical program, which rewards employees who have been with us for seven years with three months of paid time off, to do whatever they choose. We also allow employees to cash out their sabbatical as bonus pay. From remodeled kitchens to finally taking the family to Europe to enjoying an entire summer at the cabin without having to work, our consultants know what they need to make the most of the sabbatical benefit. We keep it flexible, consistent, and fair—and let them figure the rest out for themselves!

TAKEAWAY: Money is better than poverty, if only for financial reasons.
—WOODY ALLEN, *THE INSANITY DEFENSE*

CHAPTER 3

Hiring: The First Step to Building a High-Performance Team

23 HIRING SLOWLY

Building a great team starts with finding great people. Top firms spend an inordinate amount of time recruiting. One worldwide executive recruiting firm, Egon Zehnder International, conducts between 25 and 40 interviews per hire!

Most of us don't have the time or resources to put job candidates through such a rigorous recruiting process. We can, however, take the time to check out a potential new employee thoroughly before asking him or her to join our team. If you're wowed by someone's technical prowess but concerned about his or her honesty or attitude, don't risk it. When we have justified hiring someone—usually in response to an especially heavy workload—the person may have provided short-term relief but did not work out in the long term.

TAKEAWAY: Avoid hasty hires. While it may seem like a simple solution in the short term, you'll end up paying more and spending more time on the process in the long run, since employees hired in a hurry rarely make a good fit.

24 HAVING A PROCESS

You probably wouldn't choose a college for your kid, or even a new car for yourself, without doing diligent research. Your process would include talking with many people, doing some Internet sleuthing, keeping a spreadsheet showing key comparative data, and the like. Hiring a new employee requires the same diligence. Here are some best practices:

» To ensure the best hiring result, use consistent questions that all candidates must answer. You'll find it will be much easier to compare candidates if you have an apples-to-apples set of responses.

» When interviewing the same candidate multiple times, vary the settings. For example, if the potential employee will have substantial client contact or need to interact with top management, take him or her to lunch to observe social skills and table manners. It's also smart to involve multiple people from different parts of the organization in the process. At Intertech, the final in-person interview includes meeting with two of our employees for a team interview.

» Use LinkedIn to find common connections, which may help you learn more about candidates from people you already know and trust.

The hiring process is designed primarily to elicit important information from job candidates. It's also important, however, to provide clear information about your organization's culture, values, and expectations. When the process is done correctly, weak prospects drop out because they've learned enough about your company to realize it will not be a good fit, saving valuable time and money for all involved. We've taken this part of the hiring process a step further by creating the Intertech Hiring Guide on our website, which describes everything a prospect should know about our company before making a decision to join us.

TAKEAWAY: A thorough, consistently applied hiring process will increase your odds of finding solid employees who fit your culture.

☁ D4, D5 & D6

25 VERIFYING THE STORY

Hiring someone is a highly human interaction. After all, it's a matter of people coming together and making a decision to spend 40-plus hours a week together well into the future. It's easy to let emotions, especially positive ones, tempt you to skip your due diligence before offering a job to someone who appears ideal.

Here's my advice: don't let this happen to you. No matter how impressive someone appears to be, you should always call his or her three most recent employers and ask questions that get the real story. Ask, "What did Bill do?" instead of, "Bill said he was a project manager who oversaw 20 employees. Is this true?" Open-ended questions ensure that you will get a more complete and accurate description of the candidate's past job responsibilities and performance (some companies, however, maintain a strict HR policy of only confirming the dates of employment and the job titles a person had while employed there).

It also makes sense to get a professional outside assessment of your leading candidates. We spend about $350 per assessment, which provides us with an extensive overview of the candidate's personality and allows us to decide whether the person will fit with our culture. We compare the candidates' results to the top 10 percent of our consultants who took this same assessment to create our "gold standard." If $350 per candidate sounds expensive, think about the costs (both time and money) involved in a bad hire. Also, candidates are typically hired based on skill and fired because of personality.

TAKEAWAY: There are three places where you don't necessarily see someone's true personality: on a first date, at church, and at a job interview. Increase your odds of hiring someone whose personality, values, and work ethic match your own by thoroughly checking him or her out before you extend an offer of employment.

☁ D7

26 WATCHING OUT FOR BIAS

To improve your interviews with job candidates, be aware of your own biases. Author Malcolm Gladwell, in his bestseller *Blink*, chronicles the tendency we humans have to make snap judgments (in the *blink* of an eye) based on a person's appearance, eye color, or whether he or she reminds us of someone else. Most of us don't even realize we make decisions about others based on such shallow "information," which is why we need systems to override our natural predisposition to size someone up unconsciously and subjectively. Similarly, pay attention to clues that the candidate has negative biases, as we did when we interviewed someone who refused to make eye contact with one of our female employees.

Here's a tip for keeping biases in check. Make a note of your initial impressions and then set that aside. Try to keep your mind open as you learn more about the potential candidate and be willing to alter your original impression. Your goal should be to keep your initial impressions from outweighing other evidence about the person gleaned from a rigorous hiring process.

TAKEAWAY: It's human nature to size someone up in the blink of an eye, but savvy hiring managers consciously set their initial impressions aside and take the time to assess a candidate thoroughly before making a decision.

 D8

27 HIRING TOP PERFORMERS ONLY

Maybe this sounds like a tall order (especially if times are good and great employees are hard to find). Regardless of the business climate, making a commitment to only hire top performers is a strategy worth pursuing. It's the only way to ensure that you can deliver the best service or product to your customers, and it's the only way I know to increase the odds of winning, especially in an age of global competition. If you think you can get by with mediocre employees, you'll soon see your profit margins eroding, since the only way you'll be able to compete is to lower prices.

It pays to be picky. By this I mean, only hire people you rate a 9 or 10 on a 10-point scale. In my industry, when looking at the spectrum of programming performance, data show that a top programmer will be 100 times more productive than a bottom programmer (Bryan, 2012)! Great performers are rarely unemployed or desperate for work. For this reason, it's important to build a virtual bench of possible candidates who are exceptional at their jobs and who are happy in their current positions. Eventually, things may change, and they will be interested in new opportunities. Conversely, if a top performer leaves your organization on good terms and later wants to return, don't hesitate to take him or her back. This sends a powerful message to everyone about your company being a great place to work.

TAKEAWAY: Although it takes time and patience on the front end to find and recruit top performers, you'll get this investment back with hefty dividends over time.

28 GETTING INSIDE THEIR HEADS

When you've found a top-performing candidate whose skills, personality, and values fit with your organization, it's time to negotiate an offer.

I believe in the guidance given in Marcus Buckingham and Curt Coffman's book *First, Break All the Rules*, which advises that people be treated candidly. When talking with a serious candidate, find out what's most important to him or her by asking up front—is it time off, telecommuting, money, or something else? Take that into consideration when you make your offer.

Of course, there are no guarantees that candor will result in a happily-ever-after scenario. We've had experienced executives demand significant pay, bonus, and benefit packages. In some cases, we've agreed. In a few of those cases, we later let them go. There is no entitlement. If someone demands a lot, a lot should be expected of them. If they don't deliver what they promised, then they need to be let go. Conversely, we've had executives who were well paid and who also delivered.

TAKEAWAY: Understand what a potential employee values before making an offer. If someone expects a lot, you should expect a lot in return.

29 MAKING A CLEAR, TIME-SENSITIVE OFFER

When negotiating an offer, clarity and a deadline are essential. In negotiations, the person with the least amount of interest has the most power. When you've presented your offer, don't hound the candidate. It makes you seem desperate. If the candidate starts making hefty demands, think hard about whether this person will fit in your organization over the long term. If you agree to bonuses and other perks, make sure the person understands what you expect in return.

Here are some more tips:

» If you require employees to sign a noncompete agreement, remember that you must disclose that at the same time you make the offer.

» Put an expiration date on the offer. Give the candidate a reasonable amount of time to make a decision, but for everyone's sake, provide a definite end date on the offer consideration period.

» If you decide to pass on a candidate, succinctly thank the person for his or her time and frame the rejection letter correctly by stating, "At this time, given our interview process, we are choosing to proceed with other candidates." This makes the rejection clean and gives the candidate no opening to try to change your mind.

TAKEAWAY: Once you've presented a fair offer with a clear deadline attached, give the candidate a reasonable amount of time to make the decision.

☁ D9

30 SETTING THE TONE QUICKLY

As anyone who has ever had an awkward first date knows, first impressions matter. Likewise, the amount of effort you put into effectively bringing someone new into your organization plays a significant role in whether or not he or she becomes a long-term employee.

At Intertech, we send a floral arrangement to a new employee's home upon acceptance of our offer, with a note of welcome. The week before he or she starts, we send an email explaining what to expect the first week.

Beyond the obvious orientation activities—lunch, HR forms, and meeting other employees—quickly set the tone by telling the new person about your company's history, particularly through anecdotes and personal observations. This can be more challenging at large and long-established corporations, but even in those organizations, mentors can tell new employees about their own relevant work experiences to make the culture come alive. Instead of showing a half day's worth of slides about our history, we ask new employees what they'd like to hear about, and we share stories about the company's milestones. Along with history, we share where we're headed, our values, our guiding principles, and most importantly, how the employee fits into our future.

TAKEAWAY: You only get one chance to make a first impression. Take the time and care to communicate with new employees, letting them know you're confident that they will quickly become valued members of your team.

☁ DIO

31 | CHECKING IN REGULARLY

Successfully launching a new employee means checking in at regular intervals to see how things are going. I recommend checking in after the person has been on the job for 30, 60, and 90 days. These are informal opportunities to see how things are going and ask whether the employee has clear direction on what he or she should be doing. We also ask whether he or she needs any tools or training and, most importantly, whether there is anything else we should be aware of or anything he or she would like to discuss.

Check-ins provide a one-on-one opportunity for employees to share thoughts and concerns. They also convey to employees how important they are and that you want them to succeed. Most of the time, check-ins result in an "all is well," but the check-in can catch exceptions early, before larger problems arise.

TAKEAWAY: Regular, informal check-ins with new employees let them know you are committed to their success. They also allow you to fix early problems before they fester into major issues.

☁ DII

32 BEING PATIENT

With introductions and administrative formalities out of the way, it's time for your new team member to roll up his or her proverbial sleeves and get to work. Understandably, your expectations are high. You're finally going to see this genius in action!

Take a deep breath and repeat this three times: "A person who never makes mistakes never makes anything." With software, and probably every other creative endeavor in the world, a poor first draft is almost a requirement. Just expect it. Actually, do more than that. Give your new employees support and encouragement—you know they're capable of getting it right.

Remember when you were on the other end of the equation—when you were a newbie. In my case, I'll never forget the time my teenage self accidently ruined the engine in my dad's truck. Instead of losing his temper, my dad reminded me that the only person who never makes a mistake is the one who never does anything at all. That powerful lesson has helped me give the same grace to others who make honest mistakes while truly trying to do their best.

TAKEAWAY: Nothing of value is created without time and effort. Be patient with new employees and communicate your confidence in their abilities. People usually live up or down to our expectations.

CHAPTER 4

Leading and Growing Team Members

33 KEEPING THEM MOTIVATED

After a reasonable period of adjustment, don't be afraid to push employees beyond their professional comfort zones. Motivated technical employees want to build their skills by working with high-profile companies on challenging assignments. Build a specific learning goal into every employee's performance plan at the beginning of each year. At Intertech, everyone has three to five goals that tie in with the company's overall goal; one of those goals explicitly relates to learning. We also encourage less experienced employees to sign up for special projects that can help them develop skills while also creating something we can use internally. In addition to building their skill sets, they earn a financial bonus for doing these projects. Most importantly, our employees become more skilled, but not at the expense of our clients.

TAKEAWAY: Everyone needs to learn new skills to stay motivated. Find ways for all your team members to develop professionally and give them incentives, such as performance goals and even financial bonuses, to embrace these opportunities.

☁ DI2

34 PROVIDING WORK THAT MATTERS

To be satisfied at work, people need to stay challenged and to believe they're using their strengths in ways that matter. As simple as this sounds, a whopping 80 percent of US workers do not think they use their strengths every day. Moreover, the longer someone stays at a firm, the less likely they are to say that they use their strengths on a daily basis (Gallup, 2013).

As managers, we need to understand what people need, and we must balance their needs with the needs of our company or clients. Most people need to know how they rate compared to others. They also need to know how they fit within the overall organization. Mostly, though, they need to know that the work they are doing is important—that it matters.

TAKEAWAY: To keep employees motivated, provide challenging work that is important.

35 HELPING TO AVOID BURNOUT

Need a recipe to ensure that your high-talent/ high-need-for-achievement employees burn out? Give them a repetitive task with significant time pressure and no end date. This is the classic definition of boring, stress-inducing work. A steady diet of it ensures that your top performers will seek relief by finding more interesting work elsewhere.

Of course, not every project allows our technical professionals to use emerging technology in cutting-edge ways. When someone is working on a boring assignment, we do three things to help him or her deal with the situation:

» We verbally recognize the nature of the task and express our gratitude that the person is doing it.

» We give him or her a chance to take on a more interesting additional assignment or offer to provide a training opportunity.

» We put a time cap on it; people can endure almost anything if they know when it will end. If you're unsure how long someone can endure a dreadful assignment, ask him or her.

We don't ask anyone to repeatedly take on boring, repetitive tasks. Occasionally this approach has meant that Intertech has passed on lucrative assignments that would have driven our people to distraction. It's a tough call but one you must be willing to make if you're committed to attracting and retaining the very best people in your industry.

TAKEAWAY: **Don't expect top performers to do boring, repetitive work. If they must do mind-numbing work on rare occasions, help them survive by expressing your thanks, giving them something else to do to keep their minds engaged, and letting them know when the boring work will be over.**

36 ASSESSING RESULTS CLEARLY

Professionals expect clarity in performance appraisals and promotions. Make sure the expectations are set clearly from the very first day, and give frequent feedback along the way. We've adopted the Dale Carnegie Key Result Areas (KRAs) approach to talent management. We use the following questions:

> » **What is the purpose of my job?** This answer should be extremely simple, such as "selling our services."
>
> » **What do I need to do to make it happen?** For someone in sales, the answer might be "call 100 potential clients every day."
>
> » **What tools do I need to be successful?** For a salesperson, training in phone skills or negotiation techniques might be in order.
>
> » **How do I know when results have been achieved?** Again, in our sales example, reaching a specified dollar amount would be an objective measure of goal achievement.

TAKEAWAY: A good talent management system is forward-looking, has clear and objective performance standards, and allows the employee to state if they need tools or training to reach the goal.

☁ DI3

37 IDENTIFYING THE SAINTS, DOGS, AND STARS

How you operate at the fringe of your organization strongly impacts your core employees. To keep morale and motivation high, it's essential to identify your top performers, as well as those who need to improve and those who need to be shown the door.

There's a shorthand code for these three groups of employees.

- » **Saints:** those who may be a great fit with our culture but who are poor performers.
- » **Dogs:** those who score high on the performance scale but who are a poor cultural fit with Intertech (they tend to be extraordinarily arrogant).
- » **Stars:** those fantastic individuals who are both high performers and a good fit with our cultural values.

Not surprisingly, our response to Saints and Dogs is the same: shape up or ship out. Stars, however, are given extra incentives to remain long-term members of our organization.

TAKEAWAY: Not all employees fit neatly into the Saints, Dogs, or Stars categories. Most folks fall somewhere in the middle. How you treat the people who obviously qualify as Saints, Dogs, or Stars, however, will speak volumes to the rest of your team about expectations, rewards, and the consequences of living up—or not—to your company values.

38 FIRING QUICKLY

Firing someone is the worst part of a manager's job. It's also one of the most important aspects of what leaders must do. I believe organizations succeed or fail based largely on whom they employ—as well as whom they fire. While this may sound heartless, the survival of an organization and the livelihood of its clients and employees are at stake.

Sadly, most employees are not fired because they lack the technical skills to perform well. Typically, they have problems with emotional intelligence (author Daniel Goleman has written extensively on this topic). In other words, their personality or people skills are a poor fit with our cultural expectations. Someone with top skills who alienates clients or teammates through arrogance or bullying, for example, is not an asset. The same is true for those salt-of-the-earth types who just can't get anything done.

Showing these people the door quickly is essential. It's best to have two people from the firm present during a firing. A legal separation agreement may be a good idea, particularly if severance pay is involved (talk to your attorney to see what makes the most sense for your organization). Quickly pay a fired employee for all hours worked, any unreimbursed expenses, and any unused vacation (you want this to be a clean break). Finally, be mentally prepared for the person to promise he or she will change. This should not influence your decision to let him or her go.

TAKEAWAY: There should be a small delta between what you say you are and what you really are as an organization. Keeping employees who don't perform or don't fit your company values risks bringing down the whole ship.

⬇ DI4

39 KNOWING WHAT MATTERS

Ever heard the maxim, "If we don't stand for something, we will fall for anything"? The wisdom it communicates applies equally well to individuals and organizations. We all need to be clear about our core beliefs and purpose; otherwise we can be blown off course by the latest fads or, worse, come to believe that we don't matter.

I learned this lesson during my first postcollege job. I was working for one of the top information technology firms in the Twin Cities. Despite my motivation to add value, a well-meaning manager told me I didn't need to expend extra energy on my work. In essence, the company was so big that there was no need for any one person to shoulder any additional effort. That was the moment I found my purpose: I knew I wanted my efforts to matter. Intertech was founded quickly thereafter.

A company's purpose should be clear and unchanging. Intertech's purpose is "to create a place where people matter, and where our partners' businesses are improved through technology."

TAKEAWAY: Building a great organization, whether it's a small company or a division within a large company, means knowing what matters. A company's purpose should be clear and unchanging.

CHAPTER 5

Outsmarting and Outplanning the Competition with Strategy

40 INVOLVING THE TEAM IN DEFINING VALUES

Like your purpose, your values should be rock solid and unchanging. Most likely, your organizational values are already in operation. Think of the company values as an invisible hand guiding interactions between customers, employees, and vendors.

To be most effective at guiding interactions, values should be identified concretely. At our company, we articulated our values many years ago through the "Mars Group" exercise created by business expert and author Jim Collins. In essence, all employees were asked to pick the handful of colleagues who were the best exemplars of the organization's core values; these were the employees who could recreate the organization on another planet. Next, everyone came up with three adjectives that best described the nominees. By sorting through the adjectives, we were eventually able to find the most common values: positive attitude, commitment to deliver, and professional excellence.

TAKEAWAY: Values are present in all organizations. Effective companies make a conscious effort to identify them and ask employees to be part of this important process.

41 MAKING VALUES DIFFERENTIATORS

Values are most useful as an organizational compass when they differentiate your company from your competitors. In addition to positive attitude, commitment to deliver, and professional excellence, our employees identified honesty and teamwork as two other core values at Intertech. We were gratified to learn that employees were nearly unanimous in their agreement that these five values were most reflective of our company's culture.

According to Jim Collins and other business experts, however, company values must represent a point of difference to be meaningful. So we took another hard look at our values and determined that the first three—attitude, commitment, and excellence—truly set us apart from our competitors. These three values guide Intertech to this day.

TAKEAWAY: Identify the values that truly set your company apart from its competitors.

42 ARTICULATING YOUR VALUES EARLY AND OFTEN

Like anything we care about, we must continually reinforce our commitment. No one tells his or her spouse "I love you" exactly once and remains happily married! I believe it's just as important to verbally communicate company values on a regular basis.

At Intertech, we articulate our values with the following statements:

» **Attitude:** Each day we choose our attitude. Attitude is contagious. For others to be positive, excited, and inspired, we must be so.
» **Commitment:** As a team, we deliver. We demand more of ourselves than others could ask.
» **Excellence:** We're committed to providing a world-class customer experience that results in world-class customer satisfaction.

When someone is called an "ACE" at Intertech, it's more than just a fleeting comment or a gratuitous pat on the back. ACE is the acronym for our values: attitude, commitment, and excellence. It's also the name of a program we've put in place to make our values come alive every day. We've put thought into developing the program, and the results have paid off in the form of revenues that exceed expectations, satisfied customers, and very low employee turnover. While less measurable (unless you count smiles and laughter), I think it's also safe to say that our company culture is upbeat and enjoyable.

TAKEAWAY: **To make your company values come alive, you must find ways to talk about those values on a regular basis. The rewards of this effort will impact every aspect of your operation.**

DI5

43

MAKING YOUR VALUES COME ALIVE

As your mom or high school coach probably told you, talk is cheap. What really matters is what we do. That's why reinforcing our values extends well beyond conversation and banners at Intertech. We've instituted a program that gives employees an important way to help keep the values alive and top of mind. It's called ACE, and it involves nominating fellow employees for recognition when someone is observed putting the ACE values—attitude, commitment, excellence—into practice (see 42, page 78, for more information).

In our weekly newsletter, we note the ACEs for the past week. Four times a year, we host company-wide meetings in which employees who either nominated someone, or were nominated themselves, have the chance to win prizes through drawings. The prizes are gift cards, which are given away during fun events that also give us yet another opportunity to reinforce employees who embody our values. Once a year, we have the ACE awards. We give an award to the top ACE, top ACE nominator, and the top Rookie ACE (the person who received the most ACE nominations who's been with us a year or less).

TAKEAWAY: Find creative ways to recognize and reward employees who embody your company values. Doing this will communicate volumes to employees about the importance of company values, while helping keep them alive as a powerful force within your organization.

44 BEGINNING WITH THE END GOAL IN MIND

Planning a trip begins with picking a destination. From there, most travelers work backward to determine a route, itinerary, and what to pack. Running a successful business is much the same. Jim Collins succinctly espouses this principle: in business, he says, the "end" is your mission, or Big Hairy Audacious Goal (BHAG).

No matter what defines your BHAG, stating it aloud is essential; it's also powerful and a little scary. At Intertech, we have clear and measurable metrics to determine when we've arrived at our destination, including revenue and employee growth figures. We also assume it will take 15 to 25 years to arrive at this destination, which is why the destination is big, hairy, and audacious. It's also inspiring.

TAKEAWAY: The only way to arrive at your destination is to know in advance where you're going. Take the time to determine your organization's mission by articulating specific mission-related metrics.

45 DEFINING PRINCIPLES FOR DECISION MAKING

When organizations ponder their missions and how to achieve them, they should devise supporting principles that guide how daily decisions are made.

At Intertech, we have boiled our guiding principles down as follows:

» Dominate our market (the Minneapolis–St. Paul metropolitan area) through a unique combination of consulting and training.

» Employ exceptional people and attract great work opportunities for them.

» Be different in a way that matters to our customers.

TAKEAWAY: Your company's principles should be comprehensive enough to capture the scope of your operations, your competitive value proposition, and your approach to employees.

☁ DI6

46 DEFINING YOUR BRAND

No one achieves a complex mission without careful thought, thorough preparation, and keen attention to details. When organizations ponder their missions and how to achieve them, they should devise supporting principles that guide how daily decisions are made.

To the outside world, Intertech communicates our brand as *Instructors Who Consult | Consultants Who Teach*. This means our combination of training and consulting results in instructors who understand the real-world applications of technology. It also means that training is part of our consulting solution.

TAKEAWAY: Develop a brand statement that encapsulates what makes your company different—and why this difference matters to customers—and then communicate that information widely and often.

☁ DI7

47 KNOWING THAT THREE IS THE MAGIC NUMBER

What is it about three? The third time's the charm, three times a lady, three is the magic number. In business, the rule of three also applies, particularly when you're formulating values, principles, and goals. Three is the ideal (five should be the absolute cap!). Why three? Maybe that's all we can keep in our conscious minds at the same time. As the number of priorities expands beyond three, it becomes harder to focus. When goals exceed three, the simpler things get done first, and the more challenging goals simply fall away in the press of everyday business.

TAKEAWAY: Limit values, principles, and goals to no more than three. The discipline of limits forces an organization to focus on what's most important. For goals, this increases the odds that what's truly critical gets accomplished.

48 MAKING TIME TO SET YOUR STRATEGY

Ever notice that some things on your to-do list never seem to get done, at least not until someone in the organization calls a meeting to get the task on your prioritized short list? It's that old adage, "the squeaky wheel gets the grease." To make something happen, we have to decide it's important enough to set aside time to actually do it.

At Intertech, leaders participate in an annual retreat away from the company to set our strategy for the coming year, with the objective of establishing the top three goals for each of our divisions. While getting away is a crucial aspect of this work, a great deal of the work happens before we ever leave town. Retreat participants all complete an exhaustive survey in advance, and employees not participating in the retreat take part in a half-day working session we call a town hall, in which they share ideas and provide feedback in a confidential format (see 50, page 86). All of this information is rolled into a SWOT analysis (see 51, page 87), which is reviewed and further analyzed at the retreat.

TAKEAWAY: Make time for annual strategic planning. By putting it on the calendar, you're ensuring this crucial work happens in a systematic and meaningful way.

☁ DI8

49 MEASURING THE GOALS THAT MUST BE REACHED

As author Tom Peters says, "What gets measured, gets done." If you've ever tried to lose weight, for example, you understand all too well the wisdom inherent in this old chestnut. Tracking our progress forces us to make a true commitment to reaching our goals. Stepping on the scale each morning, or at least once a week, makes us confront our progress—or lack thereof—in a most tangible way. If we're truly committed to reaching our goals, keeping track of how we're doing along the way is essential.

To make sure your work goals are implemented, assign a key metric to each goal so you can assess progress and determine when each goal is attained. This applies to projects and teams, as well as to overall corporate goals. For example, if a team is working on a large software project, a key metric might be the number of bugs; for a sales team, it would be total sales.

TAKEAWAY: Find ways to measure progress toward the completion of business goals. If you measure, you can be sure it will get done.

☁ DI9

50 LETTING EVERYONE WEIGH IN

It's hubris to believe that good ideas only come from the people at the top of an organization. In fact, many great ideas first occur to the folks on the front lines as they're working with customers or developing products. That's why savvy managers take time to listen to all employees, ideally through a systematic process that ensures all voices are given an opportunity to be heard.

For Intertech, this process takes the form of our annual half-day town hall session, in which all team members discuss a series of questions designed to elicit feedback that the partners can consider at our annual strategy retreat. Employees discuss how we can make things better for them, for the company, and for our clients. They also consider how we can improve, as well as how to attract more highly qualified employees and class-A clients. A respected employee leads this half-day session (partners do not attend to encourage employees to share openly). He or she aggregates the feedback and shares it with the leadership team. Everything is anonymous, so employees don't worry that any negative comments will affect their performance review. The leadership team doesn't always follow through on every idea generated by employees, but we do weigh every recommendation carefully and, many times, are able to adopt ideas through this process.

TAKEAWAY: No one has a patent on good ideas. Make sure everyone in

your organization has the chance, at least once a year, to tell management his or her ideas.

♻ D20

51 | COMPLETING A SWOT ANALYSIS

After gathering feedback from all team members and
company leaders, it's easy to become mired in anecdotal comments and random observations. That's why I'm a big believer in
the discipline of SWOT analysis, which involves summarizing
major patterns in terms of Strengths, Weaknesses, Opportunities,
and Threats.

At Intertech, we perform the SWOT analysis annually at our
leadership strategy retreat. Nothing beats those big white pieces
of paper listing strengths, weaknesses, opportunities, and threats
in bold black letters. We find that this work, along with other
focused questions and answers, ensures that everyone on the
leadership team is on the same page as we begin the hard work of
setting strategies and goals for the coming year.

TAKEAWAY: Analyze your company's strengths, weaknesses, opportunities, and threats once a year. A SWOT analysis lays a strong foundation for setting strategies and goals for the year ahead.

♻ D21

52 ENSURING YOU HAVE ALIGNMENT

Once the big picture is complete, many people are tired of the process and simply put all the information into a binder that quickly begins gathering dust until the following year, when the process is repeated. Don't let this happen to your company!

Defining the strategy is just the first step. For the strategy to be meaningful, you must align everything in your organization to match the strategy. McKinsey & Company consultants Tom Peters and Robert Waterman created a useful alignment tool known as the 7-S Model. It recommends that structure, systems, skills, shared values, staff, and leadership style all be in alignment in support of the strategy.

TAKEAWAY: Proper alignment is imperative for more than just your skeletal structure. To achieve your strategy, you must make sure all aspects of your organization are lined up to support the strategy.

♻ D22

CHAPTER 6

Bringing Out the Best in People

53 RECOGNIZING PEOPLE ARE THE ESSENTIAL COMPONENT

All the strategy work described earlier is a complete waste of time if the people in your organization are not invested in implementation and the desired outcome.

People are the critical component to making your business a success. Involving your people means more than just giving them a simple pep talk. To achieve overall organizational goals, individual employees and partners or managers all need personal goals that support your corporate goals. Looking at the people side of strategy implementation also has implications for

- » Promotion
- » Compensation
- » Recruiting
- » Succession planning
- » Partner relations

The following sections will explore each of these areas in a bit more detail. For now, just remember that all these systems revolve around your people (keep reminding yourself, "It's the employees that matter").

TAKEAWAY: **No strategy is complete without careful planning and actions designed to involve your people in successful outcomes.**

54 DEFINING PROMOTION

Employees who deserve a promotion are those who behave as if they already have been promoted (they know the wisdom of "fake it 'til you make it"). At the same time, enlightened companies share a commitment to provide training and tools to help people achieve their professional objectives.

At Intertech, we ask employees during their annual performance reviews, "What do you want to be doing two years from now?" We also build learning goals into the formal review process. Individual goals and publicized bonus systems replace the "good ol' boy" network. I believe organizations that operate transparently inspire and empower employees to reach their goals. Tied to this transparency, we've defined in clear terms what's needed to become an MVP in the firm. Once a year, at one of our monthly all-company meetings, we go over the requirements for becoming an Intertech Most Valuable Professional (MVP). Our MVPs are the top-tier consultants.

TAKEAWAY: **Employees need a chance to gain confidence and prove** themselves before moving up the ladder. Management, while providing tools to help employees succeed, also needs the chance to observe a person's commitment, and his or her ability to handle tough situations and exercise sound judgment.

☁ D23

55 SETTING COMPENSATION

Compensation is another area where it's important to match goals with results. It's also one of the easiest ways to link performance to outcomes. Every employee at Intertech has performance goals that correspond to financial incentives.

For example, Intertech consultants have a bonus tied to their personal utilization (billings to clients). In addition, they receive a multiplier based on company profitability. Intertech MVPs, those who have demonstrated our values, exhibited leadership, and significantly contributed to the firm, receive a special budget for technology purchases. For leaders, including myself, a significant portion of pay is tied to company profitability. If Intertech does well, so do we. If times are tough and profits are lower, our compensation is lower.

TAKEAWAY: Tying compensation to outcomes gives everyone in the company a stake in a successful business performance. The most effective bonus systems have a known outcome within the control of the employee. And in promotions and compensation, transparency and communication are critical.

56 RECRUITING

Books about human capital—recruiting, motivating, and retaining employees—list in the tens of thousands on Amazon. They should. Studies show that top performers outproduce low performers by a significant factor; for example, the revenue generated by high-performing sales employees can be several times the revenue of average sales employees (Hunt, 2007).

With the stakes so high, it's important to create an environment that draws talented people. It's also smart to take your time when hiring new people (see 23, page 53, for more information). Once the right people are on board, make sure to pick the leaders wisely.

TAKEAWAY: To ensure a great team, work to bring in great work opportunities. Take your time when hiring, and make sure talented people with proven leadership skills are in charge. If you pick your leaders wisely, employee retention will be automatic.

57 PLANNING FOR SUCCESSION

As employees reach their learning goals, prove their commitment, and move up in the company, we keep a close eye on those employees just behind them.

We believe reaching our company-wide goals means making sure we are continually building talent. Like baseball's farm teams, minor league teams from which major league teams recruit players, Intertech is always aware of which lower-level employees are displaying great aptitude for their work. Today's second-tier player might just be tomorrow's leader.

TAKEAWAY: Creating an environment where people can grow, learn, and advance is a great recipe for success. Pay attention to today's second-tier players to uncover your future superstars.

58 CREATING PARTNER RELATIONS

At Intertech, we don't believe that the nice guys finish last. We do believe that trust is absolutely fundamental. Not surprisingly, we are intentional about building strong, trusting relationships among partners. A weekly lunch takes the leadership team away from the daily press of business and helps us reconnect on a more fundamental level.

Another way we ensure we keep getting along is via personality cheat sheets, which are personality profiles that remind us who hates long-winded descriptions and who struggles to make a decision that involves something unpleasant. This is to keep us from driving each other crazy in those little annoying everyday ways that creep up when people work closely together for a long time. The cheat sheets are the result of a personality inventory similar to a Myers–Briggs test. I highly recommend it for any group of partners or managers who work closely together.

TAKEAWAY: Understanding how we're all wired helps us work together in the most effective way possible. It's also a lot more fun. Partners (or fellow managers or executives) should find ways to connect and look at the big picture, as a team, several times a year.

☁ D24

59 DOING IT!

Successfully executing a business project, from launching software to implementing a major marketing initiative, requires a clearly defined plan that all parties understand and endorse. It also requires effective teamwork and people who are willing to put their shoulders against the work every day. Once a team is ready to execute the project, the focus needs to be on doing the right things and having systems in place to compensate for inevitable miscommunication and human errors.

Before laying out the game plan for successful project execution, though, I'd like to share a broader thought about getting things done: just do it!

In my experience, it's far better to take action than to procrastinate while obsessing about making things perfect. Perfection is nearly impossible to achieve, although it's a worthy goal and one we strive for when developing software for our customers. Rather than software, I'm referring to general business decisions about priorities. I've seen too many organizations nearly grind to a halt over a single issue or the inability of top managers to make a tough decision. Don't let this happen to your company.

TAKEAWAY: It's better to move and get things done than to let organizational rigor mortis set in as you search in vain for perfection.

60 EXECUTING MAKES ALL THE DIFFERENCE

Few professionals readily admit to being "process oriented" out of the belief that this means being uptight and missing the proverbial forest. I'd like to challenge that perception. People who can follow a well-designed process are most likely to achieve success. A 1999 article in *Fortune* stated that most CEOs fail because of bad execution.

I had a football coach tell me that failure to plan is planning to fail. He wasn't the first to say it, but as it relates to successful execution—getting all the right heads in the room to think through the problem, define a plan, and execute with accountability—it may be the reason he led the team to a state title.

TAKEAWAY: Taking the time to follow a well-planned process can add up to big profits.

CHAPTER 7

Getting the Most Out of Outside Vendors and Consultants

61 | SUPPLEMENTING YOUR TEAM WITH CAREFULLY CHOSEN VENDORS

My business is about helping organizations successfully build software. A common question I receive is about choosing the right partner, and not just for software development. Here are my top tips for doing it right:

- » As shared earlier, in my business of software development, the difference between top and bottom performers is a factor, not a percentage (Bryan, 2012).
- » Look at the firm's long-term track record. Here's a sad reality of service firms: it's very easy to enter the field—stop by Kinko's, print business cards, and you can be a consultant.
- » Make sure you're comparing apples to apples. Unlike cars or detergents, services are harder to quantify. Ask questions about what's in the bid, what's outside the scope, and how inevitable changes will be handled.

TAKEAWAY: While using outside vendors is common, selecting the appropriate vendor takes work and attention to detail. Invest in the process and you'll be rewarded with a valuable addition to your team.

62 WORKING THE VENDOR INTERVIEW PROCESS

Much like the employee hiring process, hiring a vendor takes time and preparation. When interviewing prospective vendors, be sure to see their past work and meet with the actual people who'll be involved with your project.

Think about the following points during the interview:

» **Do they ask questions?** To create a solution, they will need to understand the problem. Asking questions shows they care and that they're prepared.

» **Does it seem too good to be true?** For example, if you're considering five firms for a project and four of the five have stated that your delivery date is unrealistic but one firm can, somehow, hit your deadline, they may be just telling you what you want to hear to get the business (and will disappoint you by missing the deadline once you've signed on the dotted line).

» **Do they pay attention to the details?** In the sales process, you're most likely going to see the best side of the firm. If they're late or don't follow through on small details in the bidding process, it won't get better once you've engaged them.

» **Does their work culture vibe with yours?** Similar to having employees who fit the culture of your company, look for a cultural fit with your outside provider.

TAKEAWAY: Hiring a vendor should entail the same level of preparation and scrutiny given to hiring a new employee. Ask tough questions and pay close attention to what is said—and left unsaid—by all vendors you consider.

63 COMMUNICATING AT THE BEGINNING TO AVOID PROBLEMS AT THE END

New relationships, whether personal or professional, get off to the best start when the people involved communicate their expectations and listen to the expectations of others. I've seen new business relationships wither because the players involved communicated poorly.

Working with an outside vendor is no different. To launch a successful vendor relationship

» Define clear lines of responsibility to stop turf wars before they start.

» After clearly defining the role of the vendor, be sure to share this information with your staff.

» Clearly state expectations to put everyone on the same page.

» Choose a central point of contact for both the vendor and your company.

» Clearly state priorities when fleshing out functional requirements.

» Communicate constantly.

TAKEAWAY: Communication is the key to successful relationships. Communicate early and often, and you'll be rewarded with effective vendor partnerships.

64 TAKING THE TIME TO GET IT RIGHT

After you've selected a partner, communicated your basic expectations, and defined who has responsibility for keeping everyone in the loop, the following tips can help ensure overall project success:

» On the front end, clearly define what's in and what's out of the project.

» When additions to the project occur, expect give-and-take: add more time to the deadline, along with more dollars, or get ready to pick what you will exchange for the new additions.

» Expect to take time on the front end for an outside provider to learn your business.

TAKEAWAY: Milestones help keep projects moving forward smoothly. Even small projects should have several milestones. Whatever the case, define these milestones in the contract.

65 BEING A GOOD CUSTOMER

What makes a good customer? This might strike you as an odd question—after all, isn't it the vendor's responsibility to make the relationship work? While a vendor must go the extra mile, the customer also has obligations for making a vendor relationship effective. I think the same qualities apply to a good customer as to a good employee, a good friend, even a good spouse: trust, mutual respect and appreciation, and sharing.

Good customers

» Clearly communicate expectations. Assumptions are not helpful. Customers who share their expectations openly and early are much happier with their project outcomes.

» Provide clear direction and feedback to the project team to control scope.

» Take the initiative in quickly removing roadblocks for those doing the work.

» Share responsibility for the success of delivery.

» Work to diminish the political boundaries that can emerge between consultants and full-time employees. Along with this, a good consulting team works hard to accelerate existing employees' expertise, so they can successfully maintain what they're responsible for when the contract ends.

» Become actively engaged in the process all along the way (and get key people involved with some ownership).

» Do not overreact to minor setbacks.

» Communicate.

» Pay on time.

TAKEAWAY: **Good customer–vendor relationships require both parties to participate, communicate, and share responsibility for a successful outcome.**

66 HANDLING A BAD FIT

What should you do if you suspect your vendor isn't working out? Look for warning signs such as missed dates and misunderstood expectations.

If switching vendors is unavoidable, do the following:

» If it's a software vendor, start by getting a copy of all the project code and build information. Also obtain the project plan, functional specifications, design documents and models, and all other documentation.

» Get referrals.

» When interviewing potential providers, ask questions that could have eliminated your previous provider. For example, ask the prospective provider about projects that didn't go as planned.

» When you make the switch, be directly involved. Be up front with your new provider about what occurred with the previous provider.

» Don't wait until the first milestone to find out that key pieces of information, components, or tools don't exist. Eliminate any excuses.

» Keep the new vendor delivery focused, and watch out for the dreaded "not invented here" syndrome. That can occur when the new group wants to go back and change work completed by the previous provider—not because the work was defective, but because it wasn't built the way the new group would have preferred. If the new provider is insisting on rework, ask why and be sure to separate aesthetic quibbles from real performance issues.

TAKEAWAY: Changing your vendor midstream isn't fun. But with preparation and foresight, changing vendors won't cause your project to sink.

CHAPTER 8

Making Projects Succeed

67 USING AGILE AND SCRUM PRINCIPLES

Ever heard of a scrum? In the sport of rugby, a scrum is informally defined as "a disorderly struggle." After 20-plus years of running my company, I'd say that's a pretty good definition of business, too. In a fast-paced environment with lots of moving parts, disorder is the norm. Leaders struggle to stay in control by developing and implementing plans. Trouble is, long-term plans don't work when business survival is based on agile responses to rapid change.

When faced with this conundrum, it's helpful to think about a scrum in a different context: software development. For people in my industry, "Scrum" (with a capital S) controls disorder through a framework for managing software development projects while remaining agile. "Agile" (with a capital A) is a practice-based methodology for modeling and documenting software-based systems. More flexible than traditional software modeling methods, Agile is used in many large companies because it is incremental, iterative, and interactive.

While you may find thinking about software development methods like Scrum and Agile tedious, it offers a handy framework for general project management, which includes

» Breaking large to-do lists into manageable chunks, even as things change.

» Emphasizing collaboration and communication between the people who are doing the work and the people who need the work done.

» Delivering often, responding to feedback, and improving along the way. Not a bad business model for keeping employees engaged and customers satisfied!

TAKEAWAY: When used together, Scrum and Agile principles can transform day-to-day business practices from slow and painstaking to faster, more accurate, and more immediately beneficial.

☁ D25

68 COMMUNICATING EARLY AND OFTEN (YES, I'VE SAID THIS BEFORE!)

In fast-moving environments—most companies today—daily huddles can keep communication consistent and effective. We use huddles and keep them to 15 minutes max. Each team member gives an update and a "daily number" is shared, which measures the overall health of the team or project. I've found that six consecutive data points in the same direction are a trend.

Along with daily numbers, each member also shares a "stuck item," which highlights problematic areas early and enables the slaying of monsters while they're still small. Huddles can cascade to keep everyone on the same page. For example, if there are three project teams working on the overall project, the separate project teams have a huddle followed by a huddle of three project teams and their superiors.

TAKEAWAY: It can be tempting to forgo communication tools, like huddles, especially when you're in the endgame and near project completion. Don't give into this temptation because this is when clear and consistent communication is most critical to project success.

☁ D26

69 THINKING FIRST MEANS WORKING SMART

IBM built an empire on the word *think*. Why is this concept so radical to so many? Perhaps it's because we spend much of our time *doing* in an effort to seem busy and productive. But *thinking* is the most important work we can do, and it's key to deploying applications on time.

To get you and team members thinking

» Constantly ask, "What could be done today that would have the greatest impact on the future of the project?"

» Encourage balance by keeping the work within the workday. By this I mean, don't encourage an environment where "crunch time" is "business as usual." If you do, "crunch time" loses its meaning.

» Keep meetings, including daily huddles, focused. Set meetings for first or last thing in the day or right before lunch.

» Make meetings productive by encouraging decision makers to, well, make decisions—early and often.

» Remember, there is no silver bullet. Success is the result of a series of tasks done consistently and well.

TAKEAWAY: Don't get caught in a mindless-activity trap. Instead, take time each day to think about the project and make decisions thoughtfully. Encourage your team to keep balance by working smart during the workday and saving crunch time for the real crunch periods. In the end, it's consistency over time that makes the real difference.

70 IMPROVING THE PROCESS

"Plan your work; work your plan" is enduring business wisdom for today. Following a planned process makes particularly good sense in the constantly changing arena of software development.

To keep work from becoming erratic or chaotic, we need process. For software development, if you have consulting partners, look to them for process guidance. That said, while you may start with a partner's process, in the end, make it your own by continually improving upon it. I believe that seeking and incorporating improvement based on feedback, as well as just looking at what works, is essential for smart processes.

At the end of each project, do a postmortem. Throughout the process, don't assign blame if mistakes occur. Instead, ask what could be done differently next time to make it better.

TAKEAWAY: Work most effectively by following—and continuously improving—the work process.

71 FINISHING WITH A BANG (NOT A WHIMPER)

The endgame, the time right before a project finishes, can be difficult. Keep things manageable by encouraging focus within the team: turn off email and voicemail. Beyond huddles, cancel all nonessential meetings. It also helps to keep the work in a known state. With multiple people making changes to a project, ensure that the details are pulling together. In software development, this means building the entire application every day.

It's tempting to strive for total perfection as the project is nearing completion. Stop and ask, "Does this problem need to be fixed?" Sometimes, with small problems, the mere act of fixing the bug introduces more bugs! Avoid this by distinguishing the small problems that can be fixed at a later time from those that are truly critical. It goes without saying (but here I go) that the end of the project is not the time to solicit and add more to the project. This is the time to nail the requirements and get it done!

If a project deliverable date must be changed, don't exchange one bad date for another. Instead, get the team involved in setting a new date that is realistic and then hit it no matter what.

TAKEAWAY: The end of a project can be smooth if the team focuses, makes strategic decisions about critical fixes, and concentrates on meeting the deadline. Be sure to celebrate when the project is delivered. Whether a formal dinner or a beer out with the team, it makes a difference and will be remembered the next time you're in crunch mode.

CHAPTER 9

Leading Others Effectively

72 THINKING, AND THEREFORE BEING

The word *leadership* has many definitions. For me, leadership has two primary parts—how we think and what we do. First and foremost, as leaders, it's our responsibility to exercise thought leadership.

The author Earl Nightingale said, "We become what we think about." For leaders, this means having a positive attitude, believing in what's possible, and anticipating the future before it happens. When problems occur, it's only natural for your employees to look at you and wonder how you'll react. If you are fearful and believe the proverbial sky is falling, don't be surprised when your people follow suit. On the other hand, if there are problems and you define a goal that solves the problem, create a game plan, and move quickly into executing it, your people will approach problems the same way. In times of trials, I like to live by the maxim that "adversity doesn't build character. It reveals it."

TAKEAWAY: Leadership begins in the mind. Think positively and your actions will follow.

73 MATCHING WORDS WITH CORRESPONDING ACTIONS

As leaders, lining up what we say and what we do is imperative. Retired Medtronic CEO Bill George makes this point in his book *Authentic Leadership*: "If you want to see employees become cynical, just watch what happens when the top executives behave in ways inconsistent with the company values."

How does a leader exhibit true character? To me, it comes down to a lot of simple but extraordinarily important actions:

» Take the blame when you've made a mistake. It's the right thing to do and it increases your credibility with your team. As Jim Collins wrote in *Good to Great*, "Great leaders look in a mirror when there is a mistake, and look out a window when there is a success."

» Give away credit. In my experience, giving credit to others winds up rewarding you tenfold. It's amazing what can be accomplished when no one cares who gets the credit.

» Be willing to make mistakes. As my father, Ted Salonek, taught me, "If you do nothing, you'll make no mistakes." So don't be afraid to try and don't be afraid to fail.

TAKEAWAY: True leaders take the blame when they've made a mistake, but they are quick to give the credit to others when things go right.

74 UNDERSTANDING WHAT LEADERS DO

The word *leadership* gets overused, and often leaders can't even articulate what they do. Dale Carnegie's leadership course identifies the top seven responsibilities of a leader:

- » Plan the organizational goals
- » Align individuals with the goals of the firm and hold them accountable
- » Solve problems
- » Delegate
- » Give praise
- » Give corrective feedback
- » Treat people with care

TAKEAWAY: There are many aspects to leadership, but mastering this list of leadership responsibilities will go a long way toward ensuring a successful venture with happy, productive employees and satisfied customers.

75 INSISTING ON RESULTS

Leaders insist on results, but they also provide tools and incentives to help employees achieve the desired outcomes. At Intertech, we use KRAs (see 36, page 70, for more information) to align each individual employee's goals with the company's goals. Like company goals, each individual should have three to five KRAs for the year, and they should be ranked in order of importance.

We also believe in linking goals to clearly defined bonus amounts by asking:

» **What is the performance standard for this area?** This allows us to know whether a person is on track for meeting the objective.

» **What do they need to accomplish the goal?** From training to tools, at the start of the year when KRAs are set, we identify the activities or resources that will be required to help employees meet their goals.

» **What are the necessary steps to meet this goal?** Here, as leaders, we're helping break down a larger goal into smaller tasks. As the saying goes, "By the yard it's hard; by the inch it's a cinch."

After defining the KRAs, follow-up meetings create accountability for each employee. The frequency depends on the role. The beauty of this approach is that there are no surprises at performance review time. If someone has been missing the mark, KRAs allow for coaching and correction in real time.

TAKEAWAY: All employees should have a clear understanding of their top three to five goals for the year, which should be aligned with the company's goals. Goals should be measurable and reinforced with tools and training. They also should be broken down into manageable steps and reviewed on a frequent basis throughout the year.

♻ D27

76 SOLVING PROBLEMS

Voltaire is credited with saying, "No problem can stand the assault of sustained thinking." Yet despite its importance, you'd be hard-pressed to find a college course dedicated to the topic of problem solving. Solving problems is a daily task, no matter what role you play within your organization.

To be effective at problem solving

» Clearly define the problem or goal. If the problem is big, break it down. In the case of goals, make them measurable.

» List all the potential solutions or ideas to reach your objective. Every idea should be considered during the brainstorming session.

» Prioritize the list from "first to worst," identifying the top few steps or strategies required to be successful.

» Schedule a follow-up meeting to create accountability. If you're a leader at the top of your organization, consider setting up an outside board of advisors to help hold you accountable and on task in your role of leading the business.

TAKEAWAY: Define your problems and identify all potential solutions before narrowing down the list. Prioritize, execute, and communicate updates.

77 DELEGATING

Some leaders think they need to do it all, which simply is not true. In fact, trying to do everything yourself is counterproductive to being an effective leader. As leaders or managers, we oversee people. Delegation should be clear.

People who are being asked to do something should understand what is being asked of them, and they should have the necessary tools and training to get the job done. One great thing about delegating is that it allows your employees to grow and prove their abilities, particularly if the leader defines the necessary result but not how it gets done. It also frees the leader from daily tasks, which allows him or her to think about the big picture and whether or not progress is being made toward the goals. After delegating, a leader must follow up to ensure that what was delegated is actually being done. Leaders also reward those who deliver, in dollars and through personal recognition.

TAKEAWAY: Good leaders delegate and make sure employees understand what they need to do and have the tools to do it. They also follow up to ensure that delegated tasks get done and find tangible ways to reward those who deliver.

78 SHINING THE LIGHT ON OTHERS

While I don't consider him a leader to emulate, Napoleon Bonaparte nailed it when he said, "A soldier will fight long and hard for a bit of colored ribbon." That may sound cynical, but it points to a simple fact about human beings: we need to be recognized for our good work.

When giving praise at Intertech, we try to be immediate and specific. Ideal praise speaks to a specific action and the overall benefit it created for the organization, while the experience is still fresh. We also try to give employees the chance to relive the experience by asking them—in person—how they achieved their success. It's also great to give praise in writing (a memo or handwritten note versus an email) or in public, so the recipient can bask in the recognition in front of peers. As an organization grows, everyone needs to be involved in giving appropriate praise.

TAKEAWAY: Always err on the side of giving too much praise versus not enough. Give specific praise and put it in writing. Build a culture of recognition at your company. Life is short. People cannot hear they're doing a good job often enough!

79 CORRECTING TEAM MEMBERS— CORRECTLY!

No one likes to be criticized, and few people are comfortable criticizing others. Yet, like responsible parents who constructively correct their kids, leaders sometimes must address problems with employees.

Similar to giving praise, there are some points to consider when giving someone corrective feedback:

- » Seek to understand by letting the employee speak first so you can gain a clearer picture of the situation.
- » Be specific. As with praise, corrective feedback is best when it is specific and given shortly after the problem or issue has occurred.
- » Do it in private. In contrast to praise, no one deserves to be made an example of in front of others. If you do this as a leader, you can bet that the humiliated employee will be looking for a new job shortly thereafter.
- » Don't sandwich the corrective feedback between praise just to make the conversation go more smoothly. This is confusing and counterproductive.

TAKEAWAY: Although not fun, giving corrective feedback is an important part of leadership. Gather information and listen to the employee first, and then state clearly and precisely what was wrong and what is expected in the future. Don't drag it out and don't do it in public. And try to remember that while you may hate the mistake, you don't hate the person who made it.

80 CARING

I'm not suggesting that you develop deep personal friendships with every employee, customer, or vendor. All I'm recommending is that you let these people know you care about their well-being. It's not that difficult, and it can make a difference in your organization's culture and overall effectiveness.

It's as simple as taking an interest in others and remembering their important milestones, like birthdays or changes in their family life. Again, this is basic enlightened self-interest. Without their families, my employees probably wouldn't be showing up to work every day. And without my employees, my business would cease to exist. At corporate gatherings involving families, get someone else to take care of the logistics so you can focus on people, not party details. Always take the time to remember and acknowledge loss. In his book on leadership, former New York mayor Rudy Giuliani said, "Weddings are discretionary; funerals are mandatory."

TAKEAWAY: When in doubt about whether or not you should express interest or concern about someone's personal situation, always err on the side of demonstrating your concern.

81 KNOWING THE IMPORTANCE OF COMMUNICATION

Why so much focus on communication? Because it's the single

most important factor in success or failure. If you're a manager, you need to be a good communicator in many different settings, such as formal reviews, company meetings, informal feedback, and face time with clients or upper management. For example, providing essential information about an employee's performance in a way that focuses on outcomes—not personalities—can mean the difference between getting a high-profile assignment done correctly or potentially losing a key employee or client.

Of course, not all communication happens verbally. Depending on the study, between 65 percent and 95 percent of a message is nonverbal (Matsumoto, 2013). So if you're still frowning about some mishap at home once you hit the office, employees may misinterpret your demeanor and believe you are displeased with their performance but are unwilling to discuss it with them.

TAKEAWAY: Communication stakes are high. Leaders need to take the time and make the effort to develop strong communication skills, both verbal and nonverbal.

82 GIVING MEANINGFUL FEEDBACK

Giving feedback is so much more than just an annual performance review. Strong leaders give feedback almost continuously, in a variety of forms. Research from Gallup and Towers Watson shows that managers that give consistent feedback are more admired and respected. This results in higher employee engagement that impacts everything from absenteeism to the bottom line.

Here are some tips for giving meaningful feedback:

» Take a moment to pen a personal note if someone on your team has done something particularly well. Be sure to include specifics in your note because broad generalities do little to boost morale.

» Congratulate and thank star performers in person, ideally in front of others. Ask them how they did it so they can relive the glory and possibly inspire others to do the same thing in the future.

» An obvious way to recognize stellar performance is through financial bonuses. This works best when people know in advance what the bonus amount will be and for what specific types of behavior. Author Aubrey Daniels, in his book *Bringing Out the Best in People*, notes that we respond best to a known, short-term outcome within our control, versus some vague threat or reward looming in a murky future.

TAKEAWAY: Specific positive feedback, delivered verbally or in writing, goes a long way toward boosting morale and keeping star performers pumped. If possible, provide financial bonuses as part of a system that clearly defines expectations and rewards.

83 TELLING THE TRUTH

Giving praise feels great, but not all feedback can be positive. Sometimes we need to let someone know there's a problem. But before you jump to conclusions about a difficult situation, take time to ask questions and listen.

In *The 7 Habits of Highly Effective People*, Stephen Covey advises to "seek first to understand, then be understood." In other words, get the employee's perspective on the situation before talking at them about their shortcomings. By asking questions, your perception of the situation could change. If the employee did drop the ball, he or she probably already feels much worse about it than you do. Don't go on too long with the floggings and ashes. Quickly move the conversation to solutions and critical next steps.

TAKEAWAY: **Don't shy away from difficult conversations when there's a problem. Before you make assumptions, take the time to hear the employee's side of the story. If there is a problem, focus quickly on solutions and next steps.**

84 LISTENING

Listen to employees as much as possible. It should be obvious, but as my grandmother often quoted, "Common sense is not always common." Savvy leaders know that employees often have good ideas about how to reduce hassles, which are things you don't need to do and in fact make you less productive.

Verne Harnish, author of *Scaling Up*, advises asking the following of employees:

» Name one thing a year we should start doing.
» Name one thing a year we should stop doing.
» Name one thing we should continue doing.
» What is a hassle for you?
» What is a hassle for our company?
» What is a hassle for our customers?

When asking for feedback, it's important to manage expectations. Use employee feedback whenever possible, but when you can't, thank the employee and let him or her know why this particular idea isn't feasible.

TAKEAWAY: Professionals want to have a say in organizational decisions. Ask for employee feedback on a regular basis, and really listen. Implement employee ideas when possible; when you can't, thank employees and let them know why their ideas won't be implemented.

♻ D28

85 COMMUNICATING STRATEGICALLY

Sometimes, in business, it's easy to lose sight of the human aspect of communication. We want to achieve our objective, and we often view others as either obstacles or allies. But effective communication, particularly with customers, should take into account that we are all human and respond better to certain approaches.

The communication principles outlined below are proven to work well. I think of them as strategic communication guidelines (they are adapted from an article by Richard B. Chase published in the *Harvard Business Review*).

» Give someone a choice between two options when you have bad news. Even if both options are equally disagreeable, this gives the person a sense of control. Having control in a difficult situation lessens stress.

» Give people multiple opportunities to be happy and only one shot at being unhappy. In a study that illustrates this point, participants were given the choice of winning $10 one time or $5 on two separate occasions. They overwhelmingly preferred to win $5 twice. In the same study, participants were given the choice of losing $10 once or $5 twice. They preferred losing $10 once.

TAKEAWAY: When dealing with others, give them multiple reasons to be happy. If you have bad news, unveil it all at once. Be sure to provide options for dealing with the bad news, even if the choice is between two equally disagreeable scenarios.

CHAPTER 10

Making Meetings Work

86 MAKING MEETINGS MATTER

Many meetings are painful, pointless platforms for posturing or worse. But, just like death and taxes, they're also an inevitable part of life—and certainly of running a business. Fortunately, there are plenty of strategies for making meetings short, productive, and even fun.

» Think about desired outcomes beforehand so the discussion has focus and a logical end.

» If a client offers you a beverage, accept with thanks.

» Create an environment that is conducive to working together, which includes taking a few minutes to engage on a "people" level before launching into the official business at hand.

» Always introduce yourself to new people, even if you think they might know who you are. Assuming people know you can be interpreted as arrogance.

» Don't be afraid to offer a sincere compliment if that feels right to you.

» Remember the importance of nonverbal communication

by smiling and removing physical barriers that inhibit eye contact.

» When meeting with others from outside your company, mix up the seating and sit shoulder to shoulder (i.e., don't line up teams and sit across from each other).

» Agreeing on something, no matter how small, within the first five minutes is helpful if you are hoping to come to agreement on something important during the course of the meeting.

» Take notes. This shows you care and, even more importantly, keeps details from slipping through the cracks.

TAKEAWAY: Remove the stigma tied to meetings by starting on time, finishing on time (or early), and making them effective by using the ideas in this section.

87 SCHEDULING STANDING MEETINGS

In addition to sporadic meetings with clients and vendors, we have a series of standing meetings at Intertech, including

» Team huddles (daily or weekly)

» KRAs (see 36, page 70, and 75, page 121, for more info; weekly or quarterly)

» Advisory board (quarterly)

» All-company (monthly)

» Management workouts (monthly)

» Review meetings with all employees (yearly)

» Offsite leadership planning (yearly)

Every one of these regular meetings is scheduled at the beginning of each year on a corporate digital calendar that is accessible to all employees. The master calendar helps us all plan ahead and avoid unnecessary conflicts.

The remaining takeaways in this chapter on meetings will describe each of these types of meetings, their importance, and meeting-related ideas you might find helpful in your organization.

TAKEAWAY: Creating a shared calendar is one simple way to start implementing the ideas in this section.

88 HAVING DAILY HUDDLES: THE BEST MEETINGS OF ALL

If you're familiar with the concept of Scrum development, you already know about the value of daily huddles. Our leadership team and individual work teams alike engage in these daily standing meetings (standing discourages unnecessary blather), which last 15 minutes or less. Team members can join the huddle by phone if they're working at home or at a customer site.

While a daily meeting might sound like a time waster, this

strategy actually saves time and ensures we're all more productive. Since we know we'll have a chance to touch base at the end of each day, we avoid interruptions as things pop up during the workday. Daily huddles also help with "slaying monsters early" (see 94, page 147).

The purpose of our huddles is to review anything that requires action from others, to share good news, and to reveal any stuck items or problems. It also strengthens our culture of open communication and teamwork.

TAKEAWAY: Fifteen minutes a day keep problems at bay!

89 HOLDING WEEKLY KEY RESULT AREA MEETINGS

Every Intertech employee has goals related to KRAs (see 36, page 70, and 75, page 121, for more information). A short weekly meeting, usually about 30 minutes or less, gives managers and employees a chance to review progress against those goals. Since no one can predict the future, it's not uncommon for us to make changes to KRAs as business conditions change over time.

Keeping communication flowing on a weekly basis enables managers to help someone who may be facing unexpected challenges and to make sure employees receive company-wide recognition when things are going better than expected. These meetings also help keep everyone focused on the metrics that are tied to bonuses and other special compensation. We don't believe in surprises, and neither do our employees. KRAs keep surprises to a minimum.

TAKEAWAY: Hold a weekly progress check with each employee to discuss KRAs.

90 HOLDING MONTHLY MANAGEMENT WORKOUT MEETINGS

Intertech's leadership team meets every third Friday of the month for 90 minutes. This standing meeting allows us to discuss important but nonurgent topics, and it helps to keep the daily huddles from getting bogged down in bigger issues. If something is too big to be handled in a daily huddle, we simply table it for the monthly management meeting.

Our monthly meetings include candid discussions, and it's not unusual for each partner to have a different perspective about how to make difficult decisions. When that happens, we give everyone a turn to speak and, when possible, back up opinions with data. We then debate and make a decision with everyone in the room. In some cases, there may be a need for team members to gather more data or get some expert opinions before making the decision. If that's the case, certain people leave the meeting with to-dos.

Also, when possible, we outline parameters so the people who have takeaways can make the decision without another meeting.

For example, if we needed some new IT equipment but there were some unknowns, we could agree that if the cost of the equipment was less than $10,000, the leaders closest to the problem could go ahead and proceed with the purchase and implementation.

TAKEAWAY: Regular meetings keep leaders on the same page and on track.

91 | UNDERSTANDING WITH ALL-COMPANY MEETINGS

We begin all-company meetings—whether they're a monthly lunchtime webinar or a quarterly live meeting proceeded by dinner and social time—by reminding everyone of Intertech's values, mission, and principles. Why? We want to ensure that everyone understands and shares our vision. Not only does this keep our values in front of longtime employees, it helps newer consultants understand our culture and our future goals.

In addition to that regular agenda item, we have developed a meeting topic calendar to guide these meetings. Just like an editorial calendar used by magazine editors that outlines which important topics must be covered at least once a year, our topic calendar guarantees that we spend time reviewing our disaster plan, any town hall feedback, marketing plans, and other important matters at least once per year.

At the end of each quarter, the all-company meeting ends

with a review of our financial outlook: sales, cost of goods sold, SG&A (selling, general, and administrative expenses), and profit after taxes. Total transparency is our financial philosophy, because we're all in this together.

TAKEAWAY: Consistent communication of your mission, values, and guiding principles backed by updates on the progress of strategic goals gets everyone on the same page. You can't hold people accountable for not knowing something that you've never told them.

92 PLANNING WITH AN ANNUAL, OFFSITE MEETING

Leaders at Intertech gather at an annual offsite meeting to set goals, no more than three per year, for the upcoming year. We also include time for socializing with each other. Not only does it give us a clear focus for the next 12 months, it reminds us of why we are choosing to build a business together.

Here are the guidelines we follow:

- » Limit goals to no more than three, with one identified as the top goal.
- » Make goals measurable, so you know when your goals have been met.
- » Assign ultimate responsibility for each goal to someone with the proper authority.

» Have frequent updates to "shine light" on progress (or lack thereof) toward each goal.

» Create a theme that ties everyone in the company to the top goal for the year.

» Hold quarterly meetings to review what's been done and what's next.

TAKEAWAY: **Make time to go away with your partners to plan goals and reconnect as a senior leadership team.**

☁ D29

93 ACCOUNTABILITY THROUGH QUARTERLY BOARD MEETINGS

While Intertech is a private company, we hold ourselves to the same rigorous oversight of a public company governed by a board of directors. Instead of directors, our board is composed of advisors—but we give their advice and direction the same amount of careful attention and respect that public board members demand. Why? If we're not hard on our own business, our competitors will be more than happy to step in and do the job!

While most entrepreneurs crave autonomy, I learned long ago that no one has all the answers. I'm convinced our board of advisors is essential to our success. Each advisor serves three-year terms, which can be renewed upon mutual agreement.

Advisors are paid, and they receive stock options. They need to have a tangible stake in our growth and future success.

Beyond the years of business experience they bring, advisors also have the advantage of being outside of the day-to-day business operations. They ask tough questions and raise issues we might miss. We send them our financials every month and treat our communication as frankly with them as we do with each other.

Advisory board meetings force us to be proactive and prepared. Our advisors are busy people, and they will not stay engaged if we waste their time. They also don't get paid enough to stay motivated if we ignore their counsel. Doing so would be a waste of their time and our money.

TAKEAWAY: Accountability breeds response-ability. —STEPHEN COVEY

CHAPTER II

Dealing Effectively with Problems

94 SLAYING MONSTERS EARLY

Working with others—really, just being alive on planet Earth—means we sometimes have problems. Managing a business, creating software, and working with others involve challenges and require integrating new ideas and making concessions.

Here are my tips for dealing with these challenges:

» Anticipate problems and accept them as opportunities to prove your mettle, improve communication, and possibly strengthen relationships in the process.

» Share problems early, which allows you to "slay monsters" while they're still small and relatively easy to overpower.

» When you bring a problem to the table, bring along a few possible solutions, and be ready to explain which solution you think is best and why.

TAKEAWAY: Don't let little problems with clients turn into insurmountable obstacles. Be proactive in communicating when there's a problem, and be the first in line with well-considered solutions.

95 OWNING MISTAKES

As author Jim Collins has written, leaders look in a mirror when mistakes happen and look out a window when good things happen (see 73, page 120, for more about this). Collins calls the highest level of leader a "Level 5" leader, defined as someone who has "fierce will combined with humility." This combination motivates the leader to put the interests of the company ahead of his or her personal interests.

Taking responsibility shows your character. If you or your team has dropped the ball, own up to it. This is another opportunity to model leadership by moving quickly into the solutions phase. And be sure to take the time to listen to others. If you sense a miscommunication has occurred, restate what the person has said to make sure you understand the issue correctly.

TAKEAWAY: When mistakes happen, and they will, own them.

96 STAYING COOL IN THE HEAT OF CRISIS

Sometimes, despite our best intentions, a situation can become contentious with clients or partners. If that happens, keep your cool and stay focused on solutions. Avoid venting to a third party, which doesn't change the situation and can disrupt office harmony.

The best ways to stay cool are

» Use "I" statements to make your thoughts and feelings known to others. "You" statements imply blame.

» Take time to think strong emotions through and calm down before acting. If you say little or nothing, people don't have an opportunity to think you acted unprofessionally.

» Act and talk in a way you'd want your team members to emulate. Remember, attitudes are contagious!

» Keep in mind that others cannot control your emotions. Or, as Eleanor Roosevelt once noted, "No one can make you feel inferior without your consent." So simply do not accept a "gift" of anger. Don't respond in kind when someone is angry. By not accepting other people's anger, it remains with them.

TAKEAWAY: Staying cool when times get tough is the mark of a leader. Find ways to defuse difficult situations by listening to others, choosing your words carefully, and not responding in or to anger.

CHAPTER 12

Giving Back

97 EMBRACING CORPORATE RESPONSIBILITY

The focus of these chapters has been to help others maximize business success. But with success, I believe, comes the responsibility to give back.

Having corporate community or social responsibility is simply the right thing to do. Helping others also benefits our organization. This is something I've seen firsthand at my company through a foundation we started to help cash-strapped families with critically ill children and, more recently, to fund a college scholarship for computer-science students. New employees have told us that our company's visible commitment to philanthropy was a factor in their decision to come aboard.

TAKEAWAY: Having corporate responsibility is not only the right thing to do, but it also helps companies build a stronger community by helping others.

CHAPTER 13

Putting It All Together and Implementing the Ideas in This Book

98 RELAXING IN THE PROCESS

In reviewing this book, a friend and fellow business owner said, "I read the book. Daily huddles, recognition programs, offsite planning meetings ... how do you find the time?" The answer may seem ironic. These systems and programs save—not take—time. For example:

» Daily huddles ensure the leadership team is talking once a day. This standing meeting allows all of us to get our work done throughout the day. Whether it's an employee problem or a new customer win, knowing we have the standing meeting keeps us all in the loop without interrupting one another during the day.

» Other systems, such as employee-focused recognition programs or weekly leadership lunches, allow us to stay connected, give people the praise they deserve, and ultimately increase employee retention. If they don't seem worth the time, ask yourself, what's the cost of replacing an employee?

» When implementing the ideas in this book, walk before you run. Implement the ideas one by one. Start with whatever items you think will have the biggest impact. Remember, by the yard it's hard; by the inch, it's a cinch.

TAKEAWAY: Established, routinely executed systems save time, reduce surprises, and increase employee retention. Implement ideas one at a time.

☁ D30

99 USING THE DOWNLOADS TO IMPLEMENT THE TAKEAWAYS

This book is supplemented by more than 25 downloadable templates and checklists. These are all available at www.100theBook .com/downloads.

Use these to kick-start the ideas presented in this book. Below is the download list.

☁ DI LIFE PLANNING WORKSHEET
A template with major life goal areas, personal mission, and values.

☁ D2 PRODUCTIVITY TOOLS LIST
An up-to-date list of productivity tools with links to each tool's website.

☁ D3 THE SPHERES OF EMPLOYEE ENGAGEMENT AND ENGAGING JOB LIST
A graphic showing the spheres of employee engagement and the seven key parts of an engaging job in order of priority.

☁ D4 EMPLOYEE RECRUITING GUIDE

An online guide to a career with Intertech. Use Intertech's guide to create your own organization's marketing tool for recruiting and retaining top talent.

☁ D5 INTERVIEWEE TRACKING FUNNEL

An employee tracking funnel spreadsheet that helps keep track of your prospects as they move through the interview stages.

☁ D6 INTERVIEWEE CHECKLIST

A checklist for the processing of each employee through the interview steps.

☁ D7 PERSONALITY ASSESSMENT FIRM

The current contact information for a firm that performs online personality screening assessment. Get the contact information for a proven personality assessment firm.

☁ D8 INTERVIEW QUESTIONNAIRE

A thorough set of interview questions to identify only "A" players.

☁ D9 OFFER LETTER

A template for an offer letter including language for noncompete and time sensitive offers.

☁ D10 FIRST DAY CHECKLIST

A first day checklist to bring new employees on board.

☁ D11 CHECK-IN QUESTIONS

Key questions to ask new employees at 30-, 60-, and 90-days.

☁ D12 KEY RESULT AREA LEARNING GOAL EXAMPLE

Key Result Areas are a Dale Carnegie method for managing people. This is an example of a learning goal for an employee.

☁ D13 KEY RESULT AREA TEMPLATE AND EXAMPLE
Key Result Area template and completed example.

☁ D14 EMPLOYEE RELEASE AND SEPARATION AGREEMENT
When releasing an employee, these documents ensure a clean separation.

☁ D15 STRATEGIC PLANNING PYRAMID: Values
From your 20-year mission to quarterly goals, map your organization's strategic plan in three pages: Values Section.

☁ D16 STRATEGIC PLANNING PYRAMID: Principles
From your 20-year mission to quarterly goals, map your organization's strategic plan in three pages: Principles Section.

☁ D17 STRATEGIC PLANNING PYRAMID: Brand Statement
From your 20-year mission to quarterly goals, map your organization's strategic plan in three pages: Brand Statement Section.

☁ D18 STRATEGIC PLANNING GUIDE AND AGENDA
A guide for execution of a two-day off-site strategic planning session.

☁ D19 WORK PLAN
An action plan for executing the goals identified in Strategic Planning.

☁ D20 TOWN HALL AGENDA AND GUIDE
An agenda and guidelines for running an effective employee town hall meeting.

☁ D21 SWOT ANALYSIS
Strengths, Weaknesses, Opportunities, and Threats template for use in Strategic Planning.

☁ D22 MCKINSEY 7-S MODEL

A template and a completed example for the McKinsey approach to strategic planning to ensure alignment between structure, shared values, strategy, systems, staff, skills, and style.

☁ D23 REVIEW FORM

A form for conducting employee reviews.

☁ D24 PARTNER COMMUNICATION CHEAT SHEET

An example of the cheat sheet used by Intertech's partners to ensure effective interpersonal communication.

☁ D25 PROJECT PLANNING DOCUMENTS

A set of document templates for managing projects effectively.

☁ D26 HUDDLE AGENDA

An agenda for running an effective 15-minute huddle.

☁ D27 KEY RESULT AREA PERFORMANCE STANDARD EXAMPLE

An example of a clear performance standard as defined in a Key Result Area.

☁ D28 START/STOP/CONTINUE/HASSLES SURVEY

A survey for soliciting feedback from employees on what to quit, start, and focus on in the future.

☁ D29 STRATEGIC PLANNING PYRAMID: Theme

An example of a company-wide theme and reward.

☁ D30 THE 100 TAKEAWAYS CALENDAR

A calendar layout for executing and implementing the ideas in this book.

100 GETTING HELP WITH THE TAKEAWAYS

From high-level planning to execution on a daily basis, running a successful business takes commitment, discipline, and the willingness to continually go the extra mile. From a personal perspective, I've found that growing Intertech has given me numerous opportunities to learn and develop, as well as to form solid friendships and satisfying working relationships with many wonderful people.

I hope the ideas shared in this book will help you and your company. If you are an Intertech team member, customer, or business partner, I thank you for your confidence in our company and your contributions to our success.

As you work through the takeaways in this book, if you have questions, feel free to reach out to me. My Twitter handle is @TomSalonek or you can email me at tsalonek@intertech.com.

Tom Salonek
Founder & CEO
Intertech, Inc.

BIBLIOGRAPHY

Allen, W. (2007). *The Insanity Defense: The Complete Prose*. Random House Trade Paperbacks.

Baker, D. (2004). *What Happy People Know: How the New Science of Happiness Can Change Your Life for the Better*. St. Martin's Griffin.

Buckingham, M., and Coffman, C. (2000). *First, Break All the Rules: What the World's Greatest Managers Do Differently*. Simon & Schuster.

Butler, D. N. (1937, January). All the problems of the world could be settled easily, if men were only willing to think. *Think Magazine*.

Chase, R. (2011). Want to Perfect Your Company's Service? Use Behavioral Science. *Harvard Business Review*.

Collins, J. (2000, June). Aligning Action and Values. Retrieved from http://www.jimcollins.com/article_topics/articles/aligning -action.html

Collins, J. (2007). BHAG. Retrieved from http://www.jimcollins .com/tools/vision-framework.pdf

Collins, J. (2001). Good to Great: Why Some Companies Make the Leap . . . And Others Don't. *HarperBusiness*.

Colvin, R. C. (1999, June 21). Why CEOs Fail. *Fortune*.

Confucius, R. D. (2008). *The Analects*. Oxford Paperbacks.

Covey, S. (1996). *First Things First*. Free Press.

Covey, S. (2013). *The 7 Habits of Highly Effective People: Powerful Lessons in Personal Change*. Simon & Schuster.

Covey, S. (2005). *The 8th Habit: From Effectiveness to Greatness*. Free Press.

Dale Carnegie. (1999). *The Dale Carnegie Leadership Training for Managers Participant Manual*.

Daniels, A. (1999). *Bringing Out the Best in People*. McGraw-Hill.

De Smet, A. (2014, April). The Hidden Value of Organizational Health—and How to Capture It. *McKinsey Quarterly*.

Ellis, H. (2008). *Affirmations*. BiblioLife.

Fey, T. (2013). *Bossypants*. Little, Brown.

Frank, A. (2010). *The Diary of a Young Girl*. Anchor.

Franklin, B. (2012). *Memoirs of Benjamin Franklin*. Amazon Digital Services, Inc.

Friedman, T. (2005). *The World Is Flat: A Brief History of the Twenty-first Century*. Farrar, Straus and Giroux.

Gallup. (2013). *State of the American Workplace*. Retrieved from http://www.gallup.com/services/178514/state-american -workplace.aspx

George, B. (2004). *Authentic Leadership: Rediscovering the Secrets to Creating Lasting Value*. Jossey-Bass.

Gerber, M. (1988). *The E-Myth: Why Most Businesses Don't Work and What to Do About It*. Ballinger.

Giuliani, R. (2005). *Leadership*. Hyperion.

Gladwell, M. (2007). *Blink: The Power of Thinking Without Thinking*. Back Bay Books.

Grant, A. (2014). *Give and Take: Why Helping Others Drives Our Success*. Penguin Books.

Harnish, V. (2014). *Scaling Up: How a Few Companies Make It . . . and Why the Rest Don't*. Gazelles, Inc.

Lincoln, A. (1855, November 5). Letter to Isham Reavis.

Lyons, S. T. (2012). Comparing apples to apples: A qualitative investigation of career mobility patterns across four generations. *Career Development International*, pp. 333–357.

Matthews, G. (2015). *Goals Research Summary*. Dominican University.

McLuhan, M. (2001). *Understanding Media*. Routledge.

Mehrabian, A. and Ferris, S. R. (1967, June). Inference of Attitudes from Nonverbal Communication in Two Channels. *Journal of Consulting Psychology*, pp. 248–252.

Meisel, A. (2014). *Less Doing, More Living: Make Everything in Life Easier*. Tarcher.

Mintzberg, H. (2013). *Simply Managing: What Managers Do—and Can Do Better*. Berrett-Koehler Publishers.

Jim Morrison, (1970). Roadhouse Blues. *Morrison Hotel*. West Hollywood, CA: Elecktra. (1969).

Nanda, A. (2004, August 2). Strategic Review at Egon Zehnder International (A). *Harvard Business School Publishing*, p. 10.

Nightingale, E. (2013). *The Strangest Secret*. Merchant Books.

Peters, T. J. (2008, March). Enduring Ideas: The 7-S Framework. Retrieved from http://www.mckinsey.com/insights/strategy/enduring_ideas_the_7-s_framework

Peters, T. J. (1986). What Gets Measured Gets Done. Retrieved from http://tompeters.com/columns/what-gets-measured-gets-done/

Price, D. (2009, February 1). Unlearning 101. Retrived from http://franklincovey.com/blog/consultants/durelleprice/tag/response-ability/

Ranganathan, V. K. (2004). From mental power to muscle power— gaining strength by using the mind. *Neuropsychologia*, 944–56.

Roosevelt, E. (1940, October 30). Free standing quotation. *Fairbanks Daily News-Miner*, p. 2.

Roosevelt, F. D. (1933, March 4). Inaugural Speech of Franklin Delano Roosevelt. Washington, DC, USA.

Sackman, H. W. (1968, January). Exploratory Experimental Studies Comparing Online and Offline Programming Performance. *Communications of the ACM 11*, pp. 3–11.

Sharansky, N. (1998). *Fear No Evil*. PublicAffairs.

Stack, J. (2013). *The Great Game of Business*. Crown Business.

Tierney, T. and Lorsch, J. (2002). *Aligning the Stars: How to Succeed When Professionals Drive Results*. Harvard Business Review Press.

Towers Watson. (2010). "Turbocharging" Employee Engagement: The Power of Recognition From Managers. Retrived from www.towerswatson.com/en/Insights/IC-Types/Ad-hoc-Point -of-View/Perspectives/2010/Perspectives-Turbocharging -Employee-Engagement

Tracy, B. Quote. Retrieved from http://www.briantracy.com/files /pages/love/

Watson, T. Quote. Retrieved from http://www-03.ibm.com/ibm /history/documents/

Whyte, W. H. (1950, September). Is Anybody Listening? *Fortune*, p. 174.

ABOUT INTERTECH

Tom Salonek founded Intertech, Inc. in 1991, growing it from a one-person shop to the largest combined software developer training company and research-supported consulting firm in Minnesota. Intertech has been featured in stories in *Fortune Small Business, Forbes, Twin Cities Business, Upsize, Ventures, Star Tribune, Pioneer Press,* and *Inc.* Intertech has won over 50 awards, which includes 11 years of being named Best Place to Work in Minnesota by the *Minneapolis/St. Paul Business Journal.*

ABOUT THE AUTHOR

Tom Salonek earned a bachelor of arts in computer science from the University of St. Thomas, where he has also served as an instructor. He performed graduate work at the University of Minnesota's Carlson School of Management. He has completed executive education at the Harvard Business School and the Massachusetts Institute of Technology. The *Minneapolis/ St. Paul Business Journal* named him one of Minnesota's top 40 business leaders under 40.

In 2003, Salonek founded the Intertech Foundation, which financially assists families with critically ill children and funds a college scholarship for students interested in studying computer science. He has also published more than 100 articles on business, leadership, and technology in newspapers and magazines including the *Star Tribune*, *Minnesota Business*, and *Upsize*. He blogs at TomSalonek.com.

He lives in St. Paul with his wife and two children.